LABORERS
FOR LIBERTY

AMERICAN WOMEN
1865-1890

THE YOUNG OXFORD HISTORY OF WOMEN IN THE UNITED STATES

Nancy F. Cott, *General Editor*

LABORERS FOR LIBERTY

AMERICAN WOMEN 1865-1890

Harriet Sigerman

OXFORD UNIVERSITY PRESS

New York • Oxford

To Jay, with love

Oxford University Press
Oxford   New York   Toronto
Delhi   Bombay   Calcutta   Madras   Karachi
Kuala Lumpur   Singapore   Hong Kong   Tokyo
Nairobi   Dar es Salaam   Cape Town
Melbourne   Auckland   Madrid
and associated companies in
Berlin   Ibadan

Copyright © 1994 by Harriet Sigerman
Introduction © 1994 by Oxford University Press
Published by Oxford University Press, Inc.,
200 Madison Avenue, New York, New York 10016

Oxford is a registered trademark of Oxford University Press

Library of Congress Cataloging-in-Publication Data

Sigerman, Harriet
Laborers for Liberty: American Women, 1865–1890 / Harriet Sigerman.
p. cm. — (The Young Oxford history of women in the United States ; v. 6)
Includes bibliographical references and index.
ISBN 0-19-508046-7
ISBN 0-19-508830-1 (series)
1. Women—United States—History—19th century—Juvenile literature 2. Women social reformers—United States—History—
19th century—Juvenile literature. 3. Women's rights—United States—History—19th century—Juvenile literature.
I. Title II. Series.
HQ1419.S48 1994

305.42'0973'09034—dc20   93-25791
                                                                          CIP
                                                                          AC

1 3 5 7 9 8 6 4 2

Printed in the United States of America
on acid-free paper

Design: Leonard Levitsky
Picture Research: Lisa Kirchner, Laura Kreiss

On the cover: The Country School *by Winslow Homer, 1871*
Frontispiece: *Women operatives leave a shoe factory in Lynn, Massachusetts*

CONTENTS

INTRODUCTION

D uring the quarter century after the Civil War, women in the United States took up many new roles, and their impact on the life of the nation became ever more visible. A period of territorial settlement, national consolidation, and great industrial expansion, these years witnessed great changes in women's occupations, education, and collective activities. From the freed slaves laboring in the fields of the South to migrants establishing states in the Great Plains, to immigrants working in swelling cities, and to daughters of the middle class attending universities, women of diverse description peopled a changing American landscape.

In an era when women were mainly expected to serve their families, communities, and nation by being good wives and mothers, the range of female activities actually expanded far beyond the home. Besides women's important participation in the economy through the household, farm, and factory, the arena of public service and social reform captured many women's enthusiasm. A precedent for this kind of work had been set during the Civil War when women in both the Confederacy and the Union kept up the home front and supported the war effort with social service. In the postwar era, women's associations for purposes of civic, social, and religious improvement

abounded. As this book shows, these groups devoted themselves to a wide range of issues, as varied as ending alcoholism and preventing violence against women, helping farm girls adjust to city life, re-envisioning the dress women wore and the kitchens they worked in, enhancing women's educational opportunities, converting the globe's population to Christianity, and—certainly not least—obtaining the vote for women so they could participate fully in political life.

This book is part of a series that covers the history of women in the United States from the 17th through the 20th century. Traditional historical writing has dealt almost entirely with men's lives because men have, until very recently, been the heads of state, the political officials, judges, ministers, and business leaders who have wielded the most visible and recorded power. But for several recent decades, new interest has arisen in social and cultural history, where common people are the actors who create trends and mark change as well as continuity. An outpouring of research and writing on women's history has been part of this trend to look at individuals

Frontier settlers in the Midwest take a break to eat lunch on the trail.

A pin worn by members of the International Council of Women.

and groups who have not held the reins of rule in their own hands but nonetheless participated in making history. The motive to address and correct sexual inequality in society has also vitally influenced women's history, on the thinking that knowledge of the past is essential to creating justice for the future.

The histories in this series look at many aspects of women's lives. The books ask new questions about the course of American history. How did the type and size of families change, and what difference did that make to people's lives? What expectations for women differed from those for men, and how did such expectations change over the centuries? What roles did women play in the economy? What form did women's political participation take when they could not vote? And how did politics change when women did gain full citizenship? How did women work with other women who were like or unlike them, as well as with men, for social and political goals? What sex-specific constraints or opportunities did they face? The series aim to understand the diverse women who have peopled American history by investigating their work and leisure, family patterns, political activities, forms of organization, and outstanding accomplishments. Standard events of American history, from the settling of the continent to the American Revolution, the Civil War, industrialization, the U.S. entry onto the world stage, and world wars, are all here, too, but seen from the point of view of women's experiences. Together, the answers to new questions and the treatment of old ones from women's points of view make up a compelling narrative of four centuries of history in the United States.

—Nancy F. Cott

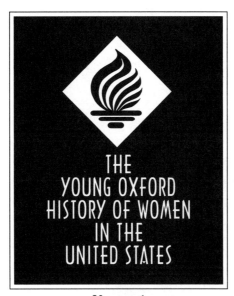

THE YOUNG OXFORD HISTORY OF WOMEN IN THE UNITED STATES

CHAPTER 1

"UPROOTED AND FLOATING": THE AFTERMATH OF CIVIL WAR

In the closing days of the Civil War, a young Southern woman witnessed the occupation of the Confederate capital, Richmond, Virginia, by Union troops. Her heart sank as she watched the Confederate flag come down from atop the Capitol and the Stars and Stripes raised in its place. "We knew what that meant!" she recalled years later. "Richmond was in the hands of the Federals. We covered our faces and cried aloud. All through the house was the sound of sobbing." But one little girl clapped her hands in delight, because the coming of "the Yankees" meant food for the citizens of this desolate city. "Now we'll get something to eat," she exclaimed. "I'm going to have pickles and molasses and oranges and cheese and nuts and candy until I have a fit and die."

In the North, the citizens of Boston rejoiced at the fall of Richmond. This latest victory meant that the war was almost over. Across the city, people swarmed into the streets, jubilantly blowing soap bubbles and snatching up newspapers to read the latest reports from Richmond. In the distance, bells rang and cannons roared to announce the downfall of the Confederate capital.

The entire North was awash in celebration. In Washington, D.C., a reporter wrote, "The air seemed to burn with the bright hues of the flag. . . . Almost by magic, the streets were crowded with hosts of people, talking, laughing, hurrahing and shouting in the fullness

The Civil War left Richmond, Virginia, in ruins, as this May 1865 photograph reveals in stark black and white. The photographer was probably Timothy O'Sullivan, an assistant to Mathew Brady.

Women gathered separately from men outside the public gallery of the House of Representatives as the congressmen voted for the Civil Rights Act of 1866.

of their joy." Throughout the North, in cities and villages alike, flags snapped crisply atop buildings, bells pealed, homes and buildings were aglow, and torchlight parades turned the night into a brilliant burst of color and light.

For former slaves, the end of the war held a more personal meaning. When asked why she wanted to leave her former master's South Carolina plantation, Patience, a freed slave, replied, "I must go; if I stay here I'll never know I'm free." An elderly African-American woman eagerly left her former owner's plantation to join a small community of freed people near Greensboro, Georgia, so that she could, in her words, "Joy my freedom!" She and scores of other former slaves fled from plantations that reminded them of the dark, dreadful days of slavery.

With the downfall of Richmond on April 3, 1865, the war hurtled to its end. Six days later, in Appomattox Court House, Virginia, Robert E. Lee, commander of the Confederate Army, surrendered to General Ulysses S. Grant, the commander of the Union forces. At last, the long, bloody war was over. But for both the North and the South, for men and women alike, black as well as white, the respite of peace was short-lived. On Good Friday, April 14, President Abraham Lincoln was shot as he and his wife, Mary, sat in the presidential box at Ford's Theater watching a play. A few days later, the assassin, John Wilkes Booth, was cornered in a barn and shot. His coconspirators were apprehended to await trial.

Lincoln's untimely death was a tragic event for both the victorious North and the vanquished South. His passing deeply saddened Northerners, and thousands turned out to pay their last respects as the train carrying his body slowly wound its way from Washington, D.C., to Springfield, Illinois, his hometown. For the South, his death was a disastrous turn of events, and fearful Southerners wondered if they would be blamed for Booth's villainy. Indeed, his death aroused their alarm that Reconstruction—the process of restoring the South to membership in the nation—would be unduly harsh.

Although he had not completed the plan before his death, Lincoln had envisioned a process in which Southern states would take an oath of loyalty, emancipate their slaves, and allow literate blacks and all black soldiers to vote. After his assassination, Southerners feared that the North would seek vengeance by demanding a high price for Southern reentry into the Union.

But in the aftermath of war, Southerners faced the more immediate task of repairing an entire region crippled by four years of war. The Civil War exacted a terrible toll on the nation as a whole; no war before or since has cost so many American lives. In 1860, the total population of the United States was about 31 million people, including approximately 3.5 million African-American slaves in the South. From 1861 to 1865, more than 3 million men went to war; this number included 189,000 African-American soldiers who fought on the Union side. Nearly 2 million white men fought for the North,

NATIONAL
DAY OF MOURNING
June 1st, 1865.

A. Lincoln

Died April 15th, 1865.

"I wish all Men to be Free."

Southerners as well as Northerners mourned the death of Lincoln, who seemed to offer a path of reconciliation and rebuilding after the devastation of the Civil War.

A dead Confederate soldier lies on the battlefield at Petersburg, Virginia, in April 1865. Southern losses of manpower were huge, and women were forced to manage farms and find other ways to support themselves and their children.

and 900,000 men joined the Confederate cause. Of this total more than 600,000 soldiers were killed—about one out of every five soldiers nationwide. The burden of casualties fell more heavily on the South. Approximately one out of six white men in the Union forces died, but among Confederate forces more than one out of four soldiers died. Countless other soldiers were crippled for life.

Because the war was fought mainly on southern soil, the South bore most of its ravages. More than 250,000 Southerners were displaced by the war. Either their homes had been destroyed in battle or they were forced to flee from Union troops who had captured their towns. At least half moved several times within the former Confederacy; others fled to the North or West or even abroad. Varina Davis, wife of former Confederate president Jefferson Davis, aptly described this unsettling period: Everyone, she said, was "uprooted and floating."

Entire Southern cities were destroyed: Columbia, South Carolina, and Richmond, Virginia, had been burned; Atlanta, Georgia, was reduced to rocks and rubble; and after repeated bombardment and two major fires, Charleston, South Carolina, was hardly recognizable. During Union general William Tecumseh Sherman's 1864 march to the sea, from Atlanta to Savannah, Georgia, 285 miles away, his soldiers—along with some Confederate deserters and stragglers—had looted, plundered, and set fire to farms, plantations, and even some slave cabins.

For those left behind—mostly women, children, the elderly, and former slaves who did not flee to other regions—this destruction resulted in lost livestock, homes unfit for habitation, and the loss of cherished possessions as well as the necessary tools for everyday life. Mary Boykin Chesnut, a Southern woman who kept a diary throughout the war, toured her ruined plantation after a contingent of Union soldiers had destroyed what Sherman's troops left unfinished. She described the desolation: "On one side of the house every window was broken, every bell torn down, every piece of furniture destroyed, every door smashed in. Our books, our papers, our letters, were strewed along the Charleston road." Union troops also burned the Chesnuts' mills, cotton gins, and a hundred bales of cotton. "Indeed nothing is left now," she lamented, "but the bare land and debts."

Chesnut's experience was only one of many tales of woe. Through-

Frank Leslie's Illustrated Newspaper *for February 23, 1867, titled this engraving "The desolate home—A picture of the suffering in the South." Both whites and their former slaves suffered from hunger and poverty.*

The U.S. Commissary in Richmond, Virginia, distributes rations to citizens. Some families walked 10 or 20 miles with young children in tow to search for food.

out the battle-scarred nation, the war changed the lives of women from all regions and economic classes—African-American as well as white women. But, in general, Southern women, black and white, suffered far more than Northern women. In many respects, the South had been reduced to a frontier: Local and state governments were in disarray; the Confederate currency was worthless; and bridges, roads, railroads, and public buildings were in disrepair. The few private relief agencies that existed were flooded with requests for help. One Louisiana widow told the New York Ladies Southern Relief Association, established in December 1866, that she needed everything.

Poverty, brutality, the ravagement of their homes and land, the humiliation of defeat and occupation—this was the aftermath of war for Southern white women. As a result, some developed a deep hatred for the North. "Every day, every hour, that I live increases my hatred and detestation, and loathing of that race," declared Mary Steger. "They [Northerners] disgrace our common humanity. As a people I consider them vastly inferior to the better classes of our slaves." Sarah Morgan of New Orleans, Louisiana, declared that she remained a "Rebel in heart and soul" and that she would never forget "the cruel wrongs we have suffered."

Meanwhile, the process of Reconstruction fell into place. Despite Southerners' hatred of the occupying troops, the Reconstruction of the South proceeded without revenge in the early postwar years. President Andrew Johnson carried out Lincoln's goals by pardoning all Southerners who took an oath of allegiance to the United

Forced to collect government rations and angered by the brutality they encountered at the hands of some Northern soldiers, Southerners found the loss of honor especially hard to bear. Harper's Weekly *captioned this scene of two Southern ladies, "Don't you think that Yankee must feel like shrinking into his boots before such high-toned Southern ladies as we?"*

States (except for Confederate government officials and military officers above a certain rank) and by establishing temporary governments composed of Southerners in the Southern states. These governments were required to draft new constitutions, but they resisted granting voting and other citizenship rights to African Americans.

As a result, Congress carried out a harsher Reconstruction by reestablishing military rule in the South and organizing ex-Confederate states into five military districts under the command of major generals. Former Confederate states were readmitted into the Union only after state legislatures had ratified the 14th Amendment to the Constitution, which granted citizenship to African Americans, and the 15th Amendment, which safeguarded voting rights for black males.

Gradually, these military governments stepped aside, and reconstructed state governments were formed by blacks, who were newly eligible to vote, Southern whites, and Northern "carpetbaggers" who came south to exploit new business and political opportunities for themselves. They were called carpetbaggers because many of them carried large cloth bags to hold their belongings. These governments ruled the South for periods ranging from one to seven years. Although some of them were incompetent or corrupt, they introduced important reforms, such as establishing a system of public education, providing farmland to some of the former slaves, setting up charitable institutions, and encouraging blacks to vote.

Daily life continued amid the upheaval of Reconstruction. Still, the defeat and destruction of the South caused much pain and de-

By 1868, agriculture and commerce had begun to revive in the South, as this lively view of the Richmond market indicates.

spair for Southern white women. "To have every thing we hold sacred sneered at—& every calamity to our poor country," Mary Boykin Chesnut mourned in her diary. "I said I wished now, as Mother prayed two years ago, that we might all be twenty feet under ground before we were subjugated." Chesnut failed to observe that the Southern way of life, whose passing she now mourned, had depended upon the subjugation of another race of people.

For former slaves, the end of the war meant many things, but above all it meant that they were no longer slaves bound to a master. Instead, they were free human beings able to work for wages, however meager, to support their own families. Although Lincoln's Emancipation Proclamation of 1863 had outlawed slavery in the states that had left the Union to form the Confederacy, he had no constitutional power to enforce his edict until those states were defeated and under Union military control. As Union forces captured Confederate regions during the war, slaves "demonstrated with their feet," as one said, by abandoning Rebel farms and plantations. Union forces also liberated those who still remained on plantations. But not until the Confederacy surrendered was slavery finally abolished. Even then, the abolition of slavery was not made the law of the land until the 13th Amendment to the Constitution was ratified on December 6, 1865.

Besides leaving plantations, the first act of freedom that many former slaves undertook was to legalize their marriages. In slavery, black women and men had married without benefit of a prescribed civil or religious ritual. Instead, they had simply conducted informal marital rites. The most common of these was "jumping the broomstick," a ritual in which the couple declared their vows by jumping or stepping over a broomstick. The slave community and some planters acknowledged the sanctity of the marriage, but the marital bonds were not legal, and slave owners could split up families at will.

Throughout the last two years of the war and during the first year of Reconstruction, ex-slaves flocked to ministers and judges to legalize their marriages. Couples who had lived as husband and wife for 30 years were eager to make their marital and family ties legal and binding. Officials of the Freedmen's Bureau, a network of agencies established by the U.S. government to monitor the former slaves' transition to freedom, urged ex-slaves to do so. But the former slaves

Former slaves were eager to become legally married and held festive wedding celebrations such as this one. The African Americans in this South Carolina photograph were probably former slaves of Confederate president Jefferson Davis.

Tenant farmers harvest peanuts on a Virginia farm. Former slaves eked out a meager existence, often remaining on the same lands they had worked as slaves.

did not need much urging. Legalizing marriages and family ties guaranteed that neither the state nor former planters could break up the family. One woman who had been married for 35 years and had borne 12 children explained to a teacher that she wanted a marriage license because "all 'spectable folks is to be married, and we's 'spectable." The teacher to whom she addressed this remark, like government officials, reporters, interviewers, and others who recorded what ex-slaves said, wrote down the words spoken by the woman according to the way she heard them.

Although former slaves rejoiced over being free, the outward circumstances of their lives changed little. During the first few months of freedom, many black women and men left the plantations on which they had toiled as slaves. Moving away meant that they were truly free. They also searched for family members who had been sold to other planters. "Every mother's son seemed to be in search of his mother," wrote an observer from the North. "Every mother in search of her children."

For former slaves, however, freedom offered few economic rewards. Southern plantation owners refused to sell land to former slaves, and the federal government assisted only halfheartedly in redistributing abandoned land to them. In fact, the government returned to Southern white planters most of the land that had been abandoned during the war or confiscated by Union forces.

The Freedmen's Bureau attempted to guarantee fair negotiations for paid work between former slaves and their new employers—in many cases, their former masters. Planters had land but little money and no laborers to work the land, and ex-slaves had neither land nor money. Planters needed laborers to plant and harvest their crops, but most ex-slaves refused to consider themselves employees of white planters because such working arrangements reminded them too much of slavery.

Consequently, a system developed by which black laborers rented the land of white planters to plant and harvest crops, mostly cotton. The laborers paid for use of the land by dividing the proceeds of the crop with the planter. A common arrangement was a "50–50" division in which planter and sharecropper each received 50 percent of the proceeds. From their share, however, laborers also had to pay planters for housing and supplies, such as fertilizer, farm equipment, seeds, and cloth to make clothing for their families. As a result, sharecroppers seldom had any money left and sometimes ended up in debt to the planter.

Sharecropping was a hard life. Indeed, for many former slaves it was not much different from slavery. They had to promise not to be "strowling at night" and needed written permission to go into town or visit relatives nearby. Moreover, planters continued to use corporal punishment to keep their workers in line. Both women and men were subject to this brutal treatment. Caroline, a freedwoman, filed a claim with the Freedmen's Bureau in Greensboro, North Carolina, to force her employer, Thomas Price, to pay her for her work. The next time that she showed up at work, Price was waiting for her. According to testimony in the records of the Freedmen's Bureau, he "knocked her down and beat her with his fist," then ordered his overseer to bring him "the strap." Holding her head between his knees, "he whipped her . . . on the bare flesh by turning her clothes up." Then he told the overseer to "ware [sic] her out" with more lashes, which the overseer obligingly did.

Sharecroppers not only had to endure brutal treatment by former masters; they also received little economic advantage. The best that most such freed slaves could expect was a meager, hardscrabble life. A black family's last, best hope for independence was its own patch of land. The son of one sharecropper recalled his family's modest dream—"the prospect of owning a wagon and a pair of mules and having only our father for boss."

It would seem, then, that little had changed since slavery for black women and men who were aspiring toward a better life. But with freedom, black women enjoyed a new role: as nurturers of their own families. In slavery, black women worked long hours for the planter and his family and had little time or opportunity to make a home for their own husbands and children. Nor could they protect members of their families from the planter's harsh treatment. Consequently, for the ex-slave woman the true benefit of freedom was the opportunity to be a homemaker for her own family. Throughout the South, freedwomen devoted what little spare time they had to taking classes in homemaking, where they learned new ways to sew and cook. Teachers hired by the Freedmen's Bureau taught these classes.

Planters, however, still wanted black women to devote all of their time to working in the fields. They complained that black women were "putting on airs" by trying to act like white women, who, to the planter's way of thinking, did not engage in such grubby work. (In reality, though, many white farm women did.) One ex-slave recalled that on some plantations on the Red River, in Louisiana, he saw white men "drive colored women out in the fields to work . . . and would tell colored men that their wives and children could not live on their places unless they work in the fields."

Few freedwomen could indulge in full-time homemaking, because their families needed their economic contribution. Most black women did the same work in freedom that they did in bondage— they worked in the fields or as midwives or domestic servants. Or they peddled poultry, eggs, fruit, and vegetables along the roads or at markets. But, with freedom, something was different: To their way of thinking, they worked for their families, not for their employers, and these women organized their working life around family needs. Their sense of well-being was closely linked to their families' well-being. One mother, a cook, claimed that she could die happy, though she had spent much of her life in bondage, because her

The Freedmen's Bureau was set up to help freed slaves adjust to independent life. It provided educational assistance, job training, and other services such as arbitrating family disputes and contract negotiations between former slaves and their new employers.

children would grow up in freedom.

Generally, men and women performed different tasks. As one black man from Georgia explained, "The able-bodied men cultivate, the women raise chickens and take in washing; and one way and another they manage to get along." And sometimes they did whatever had to be done: "We had to work mighty hard," Fanny Hodges recalled of those early years after the war. "Sometimes I plowed in de fiel all day; sometimes I washed an den I cooked." Frances Ellen Watkins Harper, a free black woman who became a lecturer and poet, shared these impressions about former slave women in the Reconstruction South: "There are many women around me who would serve as models of executiveness anywhere. They do double duty, a man's share in the field, and a woman's part at home. They do any kind of field work, even ploughing, and at home the cooking, washing, milking, and gardening."

Children also helped out. Betty Powers, who was eight when the war ended, later recalled the excitement of helping her family make a new life in Texas, where her father bought a plot of land: "De land ain't clear, so we 'uns all pitches in and clears it and builds de cabin. Was we 'uns proud? There twas, our place to do as we pleases, after bein slaves. Dat sho' am de good feelin." But some children resented having to work in the fields when they wanted to go to school. Ann Matthews told an interviewer that she could not get an education

Voodoo was an important part of African-American religion. The practice continued into the 20th century, as this New Orleans woman demonstrated in the 1930s.

because "mah daddy wouldn't let me. Said he needed me in de fiel wors den I needed school."

In many respects, then, the black family in freedom resembled the traditional white family; the husband strove to be the major breadwinner, though women also worked, and he represented the family at political conventions and African-American community affairs, while his wife remained in the background. In church, men held leadership positions, and wives were expected to defer to their husbands' authority.

But black women also exerted considerable influence over their people's lives. In larger towns and cities throughout the South, free blacks organized groups to help one another secure work or medical attention or any of the many other needs facing a newly liberated people. These mutual aid societies shielded the black community from the hostility and bigotry of white society, and black women from all economic backgrounds held leadership positions in them. Such organizations as the United Daughters of Ham, the Sisters of Zion, the Daughters of Zion, and the Ladies Benevolent Society cared for the sick and impoverished. They also launched educational projects. Women who toiled long hours as laundresses, ironers, and domestic servants became active leaders of these organizations. As the caretaker of her family in freedom, the free African-American woman broadened her understanding of family to include the entire black community.

Women also offered spiritual guidance within their communities. Drawing on ancient African religious practices, elderly women often served as herb doctors and fortune-tellers or used old African spells and charms for medicinal purposes, and their black neighbors eagerly sought their assistance. Although whites dismissed them as ignorant hired hands and "aunties," black women commanded respect and deference within the African-American community.

Relations between husband and wife and parent and child, however, bore many of the scars of bondage. Poverty, uprootedness, and white hostility trailed the former slaves in freedom and shadowed their relations with one another. Some African-American husbands resorted to violence in attempting to assert their authority over their wives, and parents, who had been raised in slavery under the threat of the lash, in turn used corporal punishment on their

The Freedmen's Bureau built schools that allowed black children in the Reconstruction South to get a formal education. Schools were strictly segregated, however.

children. But for every case of family violence, there were scores of loving couples who relished the opportunity to make a life together in freedom. And in the minds and hearts of many black parents, their role as protectors of their families and communities was indisputable. Many a black mother who whipped her children would not allow her white employer to lay a hand on them. Her new status as an emancipated person granted her the right to protect her family from harm as best she could. And she extended her concept of family to her kin and community. Out of the ashes of slavery and Civil War rose a generation of African-American women who would dedicate themselves to the betterment of their race.

In the North, women who rejoiced in the victory of the Union side also faced a new era, one filled with uncertainty. Like Southern women, many Northern women had to wait months before finding out whether a missing soldier was dead or alive. Women searched the battlefields for the bodies of loved ones. An elderly woman from New York searched for three weeks in May 1865 around Petersburg, Virginia, before finding her son's remains.

Some women in the North jumped right into relief work. Harriet Tubman—the legendary conductor of the Underground Railroad (a secret network of escape routes to the North organized by antislavery sympathizers)—returned to her home in Auburn, New York. Using income from her writings, she converted her house into the Home for Indigent and Aged Negroes. There, she provided board and lodging for former slaves and black war veterans. "De Lord who tole me take care of my people meant me to do it jess so long as I live," she explained, "and so I do what he told me to."

Other women organized soldiers' and orphans' homes and provided jobs and relief for widows of Union soldiers killed in battle. Some Northern women traveled to the South to work as teachers for the Freedmen's Bureau or stayed up North to raise money for freed slaves. The end of the war brought no end to Northern women's volunteer activities.

Rebecca Rouse, president of the Cleveland Ladies' Aid and Sanitary Society, continued to volunteer at the soldier's relief home that her society had established. Three months after the war ended, her husband, Benjamin, wrote their daughter, "Mother is just as busy as she can be feeding soldiers on their [way to] return home to different western states and taking care of the sick and wounded at the Soldier's home . . . during the month of June they fed 1,900 soldiers." He continued, "Mother wishes me to say she works so hard at the home days she's too tired to write you at night."

Indeed, some women felt that the most urgent work had just begun. Mary Livermore, who had worked for the Sanitary Commission, a highly organized voluntary agency that provided Northern soldiers with food, clothing, and medical services during the war, realized that the nation needed women's services more than ever. "During the war," she wrote later, "I became aware that a large portion of the nation's work was badly done, or not done at all, because woman was not recognized as a factor in the political world."

When her services were no longer required to help slaves escape from bondage, Harriet Tubman used her organizational talents to help needy free blacks by opening a boardinghouse. She also promoted the establishment of schools for former slaves in the South and supported woman suffrage.

Livermore devoted the rest of her life to working for women's social and political equality and for the prohibition of liquor.

Although the ravages of war affected the North far less severely than the South, Northern women endured numerous trials in returning to a normal life. For many women, holding on to wartime jobs or finding work was their number-one concern. Some women had to work for the first time to support husbands wounded in the war, and others lost their wartime jobs to returning veterans. Northern women had worked during the war as clerks, bookkeepers, stenographers, and receptionists. They also served as nurses and worked in factories. But when the war ended, many women workers were dismissed from their jobs, and female factory and clerical workers who managed to keep their jobs were paid less than they had been during the war.

Mary Livermore's wartime work for the United States Sanitary Commission, a highly organized network of women's volunteer groups that provided medical supplies, food, and clothing to the Union army, convinced her that women had a larger role to play in American life. After the war, she crusaded for woman suffrage and for laws banning the consumption of alcohol.

In the postwar years, women reformers showed little interest in the cause of working women. Harriet Beecher Stowe, whose novel *Uncle Tom's Cabin* (1852) had exposed the cruelty of slavery, was silent about the slavery of wage labor. For a time suffrage crusader Susan B. Anthony expressed concern, but she committed most of her energies to fighting for women's right to vote.

Some working-class women took matters into their own hands by organizing protests for better wages, shorter hours, and safer, more sanitary working conditions. Garment workers even formed their own associations during and after the war. Many of these associations charged membership dues to support their workers who went on strike. Other associations provided sick benefits to workers who were unable to work. A few associations established uniform wage scales and insisted that employers pay the same rates to all association members.

These associations achieved modest gains for their female workers, despite the opposition of skilled male workers who questioned why women needed to work at all. During the war, as women's labor made the uniforms that Northern soldiers wore and printed bonds to pay for the war effort, *Fincher's Trades' Review*, a labor newspaper, proclaimed, "We shall spare no effort to check this most unnatural invasion of our firesides by which the order of nature is reversed, and women, the loveliest of God's creatures, reduced to the menial conditions of savage life."

White women in the South's burgeoning tobacco industry were assigned the relatively clean work of rolling cigarettes and packing them for shipment. The factory owners provided workers with such amenities as a well-stocked library.

How shocked the paper's editors would have been had they foreseen what toil "the loveliest of God's creatures" down South would engage in after the war! From the lowliest farm woman to once wealthy planters' wives, Southern women did "anything and everything we could to make a living," according to Myrta Lockett Avary, who lived in Richmond. She recalled seeing a white woman driving a plow to which her young daughters, one of whom was nursing a baby, were hitched. "The great mass of southern women had to drop books for broomsticks, to turn from pianos and guitars and make music with kettles and pans," Avary declared.

Southern women used ingenuity in earning a living. Some women became peddlers and sold clothing, pies, and preserves. Other women ran post offices, set type, made shoes, took in laundry, or did sewing. Many women tried to revive farms and plantations that had been destroyed or fallen into disrepair. To be sure, women toiled long and hard for mostly meager earnings. Seamstresses who sat hunched over needle and thread from dawn to dusk, straining their eyes and muscles, rarely made more than 50 cents a day. This was hardly an adequate income when a bar of soap right after the war cost $20 because of the scarcity of such items and the chaotic state of the Southern economy.

Many poor white Southern families lost their farms after the war. Like the former slaves, they were forced to work or sharecrop for white planters and never regained their own land. A poor white woman's life was as difficult as that of a black woman. She had to stretch meager earnings to feed a typical family of eight or nine, and she did all of the household chores of washing, sewing, cooking, and cleaning. During the busy season, white sharecropping women worked in the fields, but at other times they added to the family income by selling eggs or produce at market.

Although poor white and black women shared similar economic hardships, they seldom interacted. Poor white men regarded blacks as competition for a limited number of jobs and tried to drive them away. Economic desperation made enemies out of two poor groups of people who shared more hardship than the surface difference of skin color would suggest.

Yet poor people were not alone in suffering the economic misfortunes of war. Throughout the postwar South, the standard of living declined for all economic classes, even for affluent planters. In a frightening new world without slaves, planter women had to fend for themselves as they tried to run households and manage plantations. For some, the work was overwhelming. One Louisiana plantation mistress confessed, "I never even so much as washed out a pocket handkerchief with my own hands, and now I have to do all my work." Elsewhere, a young girl did not know how to comb her own hair, and a matron cried at night because no slaves were available to wash her feet.

But there were success stories as well. Some women discovered new strengths and talents in coping with the hardships of daily life. Four months after the war ended, a Virginia woman wrote in her diary: "I little thought this time twenty-one years ago when I was putting on my white satin slippers that I should ever cook a dinner for myself, and now I do it every day, & am as happy in these new circumstances as ever before."

During the postwar years, Ella Gertrude Thomas of Georgia gradually became the main breadwinner in her family. As her husband sank into despair and gambled away the family's small savings in bad investments, Ella took up teaching and wrote a newspaper column. While her husband's health and hopes ebbed and their savings dwindled, she marshaled new inner resources to keep the family going. "I think and think boldly," she wrote in her journal. "I act—and act boldly."

Still, such tales of success do not tell the whole story: Thousands of women worked long and hard on farms and remained hopelessly mired in debt. For more than two years, Kate Stone and her family tried to revive their beloved plantation, Brokenburn, in Louisiana. But wartime damage to the property resulted in repeated flooding. Finally, the family gave up and moved across the river to start over in Mississippi.

Confederate men who were once powerful and wealthy, as well as poor and middle-class farmers, scrambled to find whatever work they could. One formerly wealthy planter peddled flowers, another sold tea and molasses to his former slaves, and a former general caught fish and oysters and sold them at market. Like women, men were also forced to lower their sights and do work that, in better times, would have been beneath them.

For Southerners, the war did bring one welcome result—the spread of public education throughout the region. Before the war, public schooling was not available in many Southern communities, and the schools that did exist were usually inadequate. After the war, newly drafted state constitutions provided for a system of public education. As Southerners began to acknowledge the necessity of public education in rebuilding their economy, another form of employment opened up to women: teaching. Upper-class women in particular—"members of the most elegant and cultivated families in the State," according to one school official—flocked to this occupation.

Women seized whatever opportunities they could to teach. Sophie Bell Wright, a young woman from New Orleans, opened a school around her mother's dining room table. Twenty students each paid 50 cents a month. Later, she taught mathematics to help pay her way through teacher-training school. In 1894, she opened a night school for working men and boys who were too poor to pay for an education. By 1903, 1,500 students were enrolled in the night school.

Other women also found fulfillment and professional advancement in teaching. But teaching was hard work—especially when pupils were unruly and resistant to learning and represented all levels of ability. In addition, many parents were too poor to pay the full tuition. One teacher was forced to reduce her tuition from $12 a month per student to $1.50 a month for poor students.

African-American women also taught. Black communities throughout the South chose representatives, or trustees as they were called, to work with the Freedmen's Bureau in establishing schools for former slaves, both children and adults. Although white men and women journeyed South to educate the former slaves, free blacks from the North felt a special obligation to assist their Southern brethren. For African Americans in the postwar South, teaching or getting an education amounted to an act of courage. White Southerners feared that an educated black population would be "uppity," and they resorted to violence to frighten African Americans away from the schoolroom.

But many would not be frightened away. By 1869, 9,000 teachers had been recruited to instruct the former slaves, and 600,000 African Americans of all ages were enrolled in elementary schools. In addition, four universities had been established to train black

Sophie Bell Wright was for many years a teacher in New Orleans. Initially, she taught only young women, but in later years she opened up a free night school for men and boys, which grew rapidly in enrollment.

The Pennsylvania branch of the American Freedman's Union Commission, supported by voluntary contributions, hired the teachers for this school for black children on St. Helena Island, which was established in 1862. The government's Freedmen's Bureau had no authority to pay teachers.

teachers: Howard University in Washington, D.C.; Hampton Institute in Hampton, Virginia; Morehouse College in Atlanta, Georgia; and Fisk University in Nashville, Tennessee. Besides land, the one other opportunity that most former slaves craved was an education. "The colored people are far more zealous in the cause of education than the whites," wrote an agent of the North Carolina Freedmen's Bureau in 1866. "They will starve themselves, and go without clothes, in order to send their children to school."

Teaching former slaves was a formidable challenge. Like white teachers, black teachers of former slaves had little equipment to work with, and they were forced to devise ways to educate students who lacked even the most basic skills. Most students, including adults, did not know how to read or write because laws in the prewar South had prohibited the education of slaves. Teachers drew reading lessons from the Bible and taught their students to memorize biblical passages that instilled the message of equality. Many of them used up their low salaries—about $10 a month—to buy school supplies and assist destitute students.

To make matters worse, their own lives were constantly endangered by violent groups who opposed their efforts. Edmonia Highgate left New Orleans, Louisiana, after white rioters attacked black and white delegates to a constitutional convention to readmit Louisiana into the Union. She moved to a country parish 200 miles away, hoping to find a safe haven. But violence overshadowed her life there as well. Ruffians shot at her school and students and threatened to

The Zion School for Colored Children, as it was called, in Charleston, South Carolina, had both black and white teachers. Southern hostility to educating blacks, along with large classes and scarce teaching supplies, made this work particularly challenging.

burn down both the school and the home in which she boarded. Yet she was determined to stay: "I trust fearlessly in God and am safe," she wrote in a letter. Many teachers were not so confident. They eventually gave up and went back North, overwhelmed by the task and the dangers inherent in their work. But a few teachers felt challenged and profoundly rewarded by their work—even "blessed in the effort," as one dedicated black woman teacher claimed.

Reconstruction brought citizenship to all freed African Americans and the right to vote to African-American men, but it also brought fierce reaction against these developments—the rise of the Ku Klux Klan. Shortly after the war ended, several leading white Southern men gathered at a hotel in Nashville, Tennessee. There they drew up a constitution for "an institution of Chivalry, Humanity, Mercy, and Patriotism," and stated as their main purpose "the maintenance of the supremacy of the white race." The Ku Klux Klan, as this "institution" was called, was one of several racist groups—groups that advocated the domination of one race over another—that sprang up to preserve the political and economic power of white Southerners. They were alarmed by the prospect that blacks would vote, prosper economically, demand equal rights, or take any other actions that threatened the political and economic dominance of whites. Other groups included the Knights of the White Camelia, the White Brotherhood, the Society of the Pale Faces, and the White League.

But the Ku Klux Klan, or KKK, struck the greatest terror among black Southerners. Dressed in long white gowns with pointed hoods to disguise their true identities, Klan members rode through the countryside at night spreading terror. In their quest for "humanity" and "mercy," they committed murder, pillaged and burned people's homes, and raped and brutalized innocent black women. The Klan's membership included professional men, such as doctors and lawyers, as well as merchants and poor farmers. From 1868 to 1871, the KKK's membership grew, and its members committed crimes without fear of prosecution. Finally, in 1871, Congress passed a law that imposed fines and imprisonment for "those who go in disguise" to violate other people's "equal protection of the laws."

Although most of the Klan's victims were black men and whites who were willing to share power with blacks, some black women were also targets. Other black women had to stand by helplessly

Rural blacks were especially vulnerable to attack by hooded and robed members of the Ku Klux Klan, who resorted to violence and intimidation. In addition to their racial prejudices, Klan members saw the freed slaves as a threat to their economic well-being.

watching as the Klan tortured or killed their husbands. In the early 1870s, many women testified at a congressional inquiry conducted in the South, and their testimony was dramatic and poignant. One black woman, whose husband had been elected constable, an official responsible for maintaining public law and order, testified that the Klan forced her and her children to "wrap our heads up in bed-quilts and come out of the house, and they then set it on fire, burning it up, and my husband in it, and all we had."

Other women told of being beaten when the Klan could not find their husbands, who were the real targets. Still other women were beaten simply for acting "uppity" or for rejecting sexual advances by white men. Hannah Tutson of Clay County, Florida, was whipped from "the crown of my head to the soles of my feet" merely because she and her husband, Samuel, had worked hard and acquired a large parcel of land. In the early years of Reconstruction, the terror of the Ku Klux Klan threatened the already precarious lives of free African-American women and men throughout the South.

The end of the Civil War brought many changes. It abolished slavery once and for all in the South, though most freed African-American women and men endured hardships almost as severe as those of slavery. But despite their meager lives, African-American women derived great fulfillment in caring for families and kin. For many Southern white women and men from the planter class, the wealthy, mannered life that they had once known faded into memory as they set about rebuilding farms and plantations and faced mounting debt. Many Southern women performed paid work for the first time in their lives, and some discovered through their work strengths and resources that they never knew they had. In the North, however, women who had worked during the war were often forced to relinquish their jobs to returning veterans, while other women worked at lower wages. But women in some of the trades fought valiantly for better working conditions and higher wages and achieved some modest gains.

The postwar years, then, set the stage for important advances in American women's lives, although many men—and women—continued to define women's role primarily as that of wife and mother. But the times were changing. The fiery trial through which the nation had passed would spark in many women greater recognition of their talents and abilities and fan their desire to lead more active and visible public lives.

CHAPTER 2

"THEN WE WILL ALL BE FREE": WOMEN FIGHT FOR THEIR RIGHTS

After the Civil War ended, American women had battles to wage on other fronts—for the right to vote, to attend college, and to gain greater control over their lives. As Ernestine Rose, a leader in the women's rights movement, once proclaimed, "Freedom, my friends, does not come from the clouds, like a meteor. . . . It does not come without great efforts and great sacrifices; all who love liberty have to labor for it." In the afterglow of victory for the Union and peace for the entire nation, she and other champions of women's rights forged ahead, ready to labor for their freedom. From their battles emerged many new ideas for achieving social and political equality for women.

During the war, leaders of the women's rights movement, such as Elizabeth Cady Stanton and Susan B. Anthony, had shifted their efforts from fighting for women's political and economic rights to campaigning for the abolition of slavery. Now that slavery had been abolished, they confidently expected fellow abolitionists to work for women's right to vote. But they would be sadly disillusioned—a long, hard struggle for woman suffrage lay ahead.

Their disillusionment was even more keen because the origins of the postwar women's rights movement lay in the prewar abolition movement. The two movements had been closely linked for 30 years. Just as a slave was a person with certain inalienable rights to

Elizabeth Cady Stanton and Susan B. Anthony were a formidable team in both the abolition and suffrage movements. Though they had many disagreements and even periods of estrangement, they shared a warm friendship over many years.

Ernestine L. Rose, an immigrant from Poland, was an early leader of the woman suffrage movement. Along with Stanton and Anthony, she also worked to win property rights for married women in New York State.

his person and property, so was a woman a person with certain inalienable rights. And just as abolition was a social movement that harnessed people's *collective* energy and power to abolish the oppressive institution of slavery, the women's rights movement before the Civil War was the first independent movement of American women to strive for more political power for women.

Although it did not seriously question women's roles as wives and mothers, this movement challenged the unequal social and political position of women. At the first women's rights convention, at Seneca Falls, New York, in 1848, Elizabeth Cady Stanton, the chief organizer of the convention and a leader in the movement, declared, "Let woman live as she should. . . . Let her know that her spirit is fitted for as high a sphere as man's, and that her soul requires food as pure and exalted as his."

But for woman's spirit to share this high sphere with man's she required certain rights, especially political rights, and from that first convention the women's rights movement demanded suffrage, the right to vote. Suffrage, these activists declared, would grant to women other rights and protections they did not yet have. In the 1840s, for example, married women in particular lost most of their legal and economic rights. Their husbands were entitled to any property that they inherited or acquired. If they worked, their husbands were also entitled to pocket their wages. In divorce proceedings, husbands automatically gained custody of the children, according to the tradition of English common law. Single working women also lacked essential rights: They had to pay taxes but had no voice in how their tax dollars were used because they could not vote.

After the Civil War, leaders of the women's rights movement looked to a new source for inspiration: the United States Constitution. To this end, they adopted the very same rationale for female suffrage used by proponents of suffrage for African Americans— that the right to vote was the individual's right as a citizen and provided the foundation for democratic government, which the North had just fought to protect in the Civil War.

In the immediate post–Civil War years, women's rights leaders maintained that voting was a basic right shared by all citizens, men and women, white and black. Ernestine Rose declared, "Human beings are men and women, possessed of human faculties, and understanding, which we call mind; and mind recognizes no sex, therefore the term 'male,' as applied to human beings—to citizens—ought to be expunged from the Constitution and laws as a last remnant of barbarism."

To achieve this goal, Stanton, Anthony, Antoinette Brown Blackwell, Lucy Stone, and other suffrage fighters established the American Equal Rights Association in 1865 to campaign for both black and female suffrage. Lucretia Mott, a highly respected Quaker woman, was elected president. Stanton served as first vice president and Anthony became corresponding secretary. The creation of this organization was a milestone in the fight for female equality; it was the first organization formed by American women and men to fight for the fundamental human right to vote.

Lucretia Mott, a Quaker minister, helped Elizabeth Cady Stanton organize the first women's rights convention in Seneca Falls, New York, in 1848. A woman of great dignity and principles, she also supported education and suffrage for African Americans.

But divisions emerged within the American Equal Rights Association over the best way to achieve suffrage for all Americans. Some members were willing to support the Republican party's strategy of working first to enfranchise black men—that is, grant them the right to vote—while postponing efforts to enfranchise women until they had achieved their first goal. In contrast, other members continued to support efforts to enfranchise both African-American men and all women.

The first major conflict between proponents of black male suffrage and proponents of suffrage for all Americans erupted in 1867 in Kansas. There, two proposals, one that granted female suffrage and one that provided for black male suffrage, came to a vote. Stanton and Anthony campaigned for both, but two of their political partners—Lucy Stone and Henry Blackwell, prominent activists in the prewar abolition movement—supported Republican abolitionists whose first priority was black male suffrage.

Stanton and Anthony were astonished that their fellow reformers would abandon the fight for female suffrage. For their part, Stone and Blackwell were unwilling to divert popular support for black male suffrage. They feared that supporting female enfranchisement would undermine any public support for black male suffrage. As it turned out, both proposals were defeated.

The fight for suffrage for all Americans suffered another blow with the ratification, or approval, of the 14th Amendment to the Constitution on July 9, 1868. This amendment shattered the com-

Lucy Stone and her husband, Henry Blackwell, were more committed to black male suffrage than to woman suffrage. Her views put her at odds with Elizabeth Cady Stanton and Susan B. Anthony and led to clashes within the suffrage movement.

mon basis of female and black suffrage—natural rights—by affirming black men's status and rights as American citizens while remaining silent about the citizenship rights of women. It did this by introducing into the Constitution the distinction of sex and penalizing states for denying to any of their "male inhabitants" the right to vote. It was the "Negro's hour," insisted former abolitionists—the freedman needed the ballot to protect him from physical harm and political injustice. When women were "dragged from their houses and hung upon lamp-posts" like black men, declared the great orator and former slave Frederick Douglass, then they, too, would need the ballot's protection as much as black men did.

On February 3, 1870, nearly three years after the 14th Amendment was passed, the 15th Amendment was ratified, making women's political invisibility complete. It prohibited states from denying to citizens the right to vote "on account of race, color, or previous condition of servitude" but remained silent about prohibitions based on sex. In effect, both the 14th and 15th Amendments excluded women from the main right of citizenship—voting.

But the growing division within the women's rights movement and the blow dealt to woman suffrage by the 14th and 15th Amendments did not discourage African-American women from supporting female equality. Sojourner Truth, a former slave and celebrated crusader for both abolition and women's rights, pointedly reminded audiences of black women's need for equal political rights. She claimed that slavery had been only partly abolished because black women did not share the same rights as black men. But she wanted slavery destroyed "root and branch. Then we will all be free indeed."

Other prominent African-American women shared Truth's views. Mary Ann Shadd Cary, a teacher and one of the first women lawyers in the United States, joined the Universal Franchise Association, a suffrage organization composed of both black and white members in Washington, D.C., and represented it at conventions of African-American organizations. Along with other members of the Universal Franchise Association, she addressed the House Judiciary Committee of the U.S. Congress on behalf of woman suffrage. She also helped to organize the Colored Woman's Progressive Franchise Association, a group that set out to challenge the assumption that "men only may conduct industrial and other things." The association hoped to establish newspapers, banks, cooperative stores, and a printing press, all owned and operated by women.

Frances Ellen Watkins Harper was also an outspoken supporter of women's rights. In the following excerpt from her poem "Dialogue on Woman's Rights," she explained why black men should support woman suffrage:

Some thought that it would never do
For us in Southern lands,
To change the fetters on our wrists
For the ballot in our hands.
Now if you don't believe 'twas right
To crowd us from the track
How can you push your wife aside
And try to hold her back?

By the late 1860s, Elizabeth Cady Stanton had adopted a similar strategy in fighting for female suffrage. Like Sojourner Truth, she and others no longer emphasized women's common humanity with men and therefore women's common right to suffrage. Instead, she argued, women were different from men, and for that reason they were particularly worthy and needful of having the right to

The poet Frances Ellen Watkins Harper was an eloquent spokeswoman for blacks' civil and economic rights. "I belong to this race," she proclaimed, "and when it is down I belong to a down race; when it is up I belong to a risen race."

Sojourner Truth was an avid supporter of woman suffrage. But her final crusade was on behalf of her freed brethren— for land of their own to farm and for better educational opportunities.

vote. She drew on decades-old arguments that celebrated women's unique intellectual, emotional, and moral qualities. In an address to a women's rights convention, she proclaimed, "There is sex in the spiritual as well as the physical and what we need today in government, in the world of morals and thought, is the recognition of the feminine element, as it is this alone that can hold the masculine in check."

Throughout American history, this celebration of women's unique qualities has helped to expand women's influence beyond the home and into the community. Although women were prohibited from voting, serving as legislators, and fighting for the defense of liberty because of their sex, they were obligated to raise liberty-loving sons who dutifully discharged these tasks of citizenship.

In the antebellum years of the 1830s, women used the same argument to create more visible roles for themselves: As pious, virtuous, and kindly maternal figures, they were obligated not only to raise patriotic sons but to devote themselves to the public good—to extend a helping hand to widows, orphans, "fallen women," and others in need of their excellent influence. To this end, middle-class women, who had more time for such endeavors, organized or joined charitable societies to spread the moral standards of the home throughout the community. Now, in the post–Civil War era, Stanton and others once again elevated women's "feminine element" into a virtue that would protect the nation's moral life.

Stanton claimed that voting was both a basic right and the most effective way for women to exert their moral influence. By the late 1860s, she had been a mover and shaker in the American women's rights movement for 20 years. Her staunch friend and partner in the movement was Susan B. Anthony, whom she had met in 1851. Between them arose an alliance that would endure for 50 years.

Their steadfast friendship steeled them for the hard political battles yet to be fought. In 1868, they established their own newspaper, the *Revolution*, to promote their campaign for women's rights. In a letter to Anthony, Stanton explained the significance of the newspaper's name and offered her vision of the struggle ahead: "The establishing of woman on her rightful throne is the greatest revolution the world has ever known or will know," she rhapsodized. "A journal called the *Rosebud* might answer for those who come with kid gloves and

On the front page of its third issue, The Revolution *printed excerpts from reports in other newspapers about it, both positive and negative. Beneath each excerpt ran an appropriate response.*

The Revolution.

PRINCIPLE, NOT POLICY: JUSTICE, NOT FAVORS.—MEN, THEIR RIGHTS AND NOTHING MORE: WOMEN, THEIR RIGHTS AND NOTHING LESS.

VOL. I.—NO. 3.   NEW YORK, WEDNESDAY, JANUARY 22, 1868. $2.00 A YEAR.

The Revolution;

THE ORGAN OF THE

NATIONAL PARTY OF NEW AMERICA.

PRINCIPLE, NOT POLICY—INDIVIDUAL RIGHTS AN RESPONSIBILITIES.

THE REVOLUTION WILL DISCUSS:

1. IN POLITICS—Educated Suffrage, Irrespective of Sex or Color; Equal Pay to Women for Equal Work; Eight Hours Labor; Abolition of Standing Armies and Party Despotisms. Down with Politicians—Up with the People!

2. IN RELIGION—Deeper Thought; Broader Ideas; Science not Superstition; Personal Purity; Love to Man as well as God.

3. IN SOCIAL LIFE.—Practical Education, not Theoretical; Fact, not Fiction; Virtue, not Vice; Cold Water, not Alcoholic Drinks or Medicines. Devoted to Morality and Reform, THE REVOLUTION will not insert Gross Personalities and Quack Advertisements, which even Religious Newspapers introduce to every family.

4. THE REVOLUTION proposes a new Commercial and Financial Policy. America no longer led by Europe. Gold, like our Cotton and Corn, for sale. Greenbacks for money. An American System of Finance. American Products and Labor Free. Foreign Manufactures Prohibited. Open doors to Artisans and Immigrants. Atlantic and Pacific Oceans for American Steamships and Shipping ; or American goods in American bottoms. New York the Financial Centre of the World. Wall Street emancipated from Bank of England, or American Cash for American Bills. The Credit Foncier and Credit Mobilier System, or Capital Mobilized to Resuscitate the South and our Mining Interests, and to People the Country from Ocean to Ocean, from Omaha to San Francisco. More organized Labor, more Cotton, more Gold and Silver Bullion to sell foreigners at the highest prices. Ten millions of Naturalized Citizens DEMAND A PENNY OCEAN POSTAGE, fo Strengthen the Brotherhood of Labor. If Congress Vote One Hundred and Twenty-five Millions for a Standing Army and Freedman's Bureau for the Blacks, cannot they spare One Million for the Whites, to keep bright the chain of friendship between them and their Fatherland?

Send in your Subscription. THE REVOLUTION, published weekly, will be the Great Organ of the Age.

TERMS.—Two dollars a year, in advance. Ten names ($20) entitle the sender to one copy free.

ELIZABETH CADY STANTON, } EDS.
PARKER PILLSBURY,

SUSAN B. ANTHONY, PROPRIETOR.

37 Park Row (Room 17), New York City,
To whom address all business letters.

WESTWARD.

BY GEORGE FRANCIS TRAIN.

EPIGRAM HISTORY OF THE WORLD, IN NINE ACTS.

[WRITTEN on the summit of the Rocky Mountains. Inspired on witnessing the moon set as the sun rose Nov. 13, 1867.]

WESTWARD! Ever Westward, for a thousand generations,
Civilization marching onward, peopled the Ancient Nations,
When woman sold her jewels, 'twas in Fourteen Ninety-two,
That Columbus left the Old World, and landed in the New.
Again in Sixteen Twenty. Miles Standish on the dock,
Founded our Mighty Empire, where he anchored *on a rock!*

Westward! Ever Westward, seven score and sixteen years,
We worked and toiled, and grew beyond the British House of Peers.
Oppressive taxes—wrath aroused—then Charon crossed the Styx,
Up with the flag—down with the Tea—cried Men of Seventy-six.

Westward! Ever Westward, in Eighteen Sixty-one,
Our people roused from lethargy at sound of Sumter gun.
And then our old arch-enemy went tottering to the grave,
England loosed her grip of death when we set free the slave.

Westward! Ever Westward, in December Sixty-three,
I broke the ground at Omaha, half way from sea to sea.
Westward! Ever Westward, in the following month of May,
The Railroad King Durant pushed on, two miles or more a day.

'Tis morn! on Rocky Mountains' top, whose columns reach the skies,
We see the moon retire to rest ! The sun in splendor rise !

Eastward! Presto! Eastward, let my Fenians share the praise,
When Asia visits Europe in less than thirty days!

WHAT THE PRESS SAYS OF THE REVOLUTION.

SUNDAY TIMES.

THE LADIES MILITANT : It is out at last. If the women, as a body, have not succeeded in getting up a revolution, Susan B. Anthony, as their representative, has. Her "*Revolution*" was issued last Thursday as a sort of New Year's gift to what she considered a yearning public, and it is said to be "charged to the muzzle with literary nitro-glycerine."

If Mrs. Stanton would attend a little more to her domestic duties and a little less to those of the great public, perhaps she would exalt her sex quite as much as she does by Quixotically fighting windmills in their gratuitous behalf, and she might possibly set a notable example of domestic felicity. No married woman can convert herself into a feminine Knight of the Rueful Visage and ride about the country attempting to redress imaginary wrongs, without leaving her own household in a neglected condition that must be an eloquent witness against her. As for the spinsters, we have often said that every woman has a natural and inalienable right to a good husband and a pretty baby. When, by proper "agitation," she has secured this right, she best honors herself and her sex by leaving public affairs behind her, and by endeavoring to show how happy she can make the little world of which she has just become the brilliant centre.

Ah! sir, in recommending to our attention domestic economy, you have assailed us in our stronghold. Here we are unsurpassed. We know—what not one woman in ten thousand does know—how to take care of a child, make good bread, and keep a home clean. We never harbor rats, mice, or cockroaches, ants, fleas, or bed bugs. Our children have never run the gauntlet of sprue, jaundice, croup, chicken-pox, whooping-cough, measles, scarlet-fever or fits ; but they are healthy, rosy, happy, and well-fed. Pork, salt meat, mackerel, rancid butter, heavy bread, lard, cream of tartar and soda, or any other culinary abominations are never found on our table. Now let every man who wants his wife to know how to do likewise take THE REVOLUTION, in which not only the ballot, but bread and babies will be discussed.

As to spinsters, our proprietor says, that just as soon as she is enfranchised, and the laws on marriage and divorce are equal for man and woman, she will take the subject of matrimony into serious consideration, perhaps call on the editor of the *Sunday Times.*

N. Y. CITIZEN.

THE REVOLUTION, advocating "love to man as well as God," is edited by Miss Parker Pillsbury, and two gay young fellows named Mrs. Elizabeth Cady Stanton and Miss Susan B. Anthony. It advocates "Equal pay to women for equal work." Why does it not go for exact justice to all, irrespective of sex or color, and also demand " Equal pay to men for equal work with women ?" This, we take it, would save a great many good dollars to a good many good fellows. As society is now organized, we men have to do all the work and the women get all the money. In the dictionary of Fifth avenue, the word husband is thus defined : " Husband—a useful domestic drudge ; a machine that makes dollars."

Exact justice to all, irrespective of sex and color, is precisely what we advocate. We do not forget our sons in demanding the rights of our daughters. When all girls are educated for self dependence, men will cease to be mere machines for making money, while the wealth of the nation will be doubled.

CAMBRIDGE PRESS.

A LIVE NEWSPAPER.—THE REVOLUTION is a great fact. All the leaders in the nation will take it. It is the organ of Temperance—of one hundred thousand school Teachers—of morality, and a new system of Finance. The subscription-list already contains the President and Cabinet of the United States—the Vice-President and Senate—the Speaker and the members of the House of Representatives—all the Governors, Bankers and Brokers. Ten thousand first number.

THE REVOLUTION will be the Organ of the National Party of New America, based on individual rights in political, religious and social life. It will be devoted to Principle, not Policy. It will be backed by the Credit Foncier of America, the Credit Mobilier of America, the Pacific Railroad Company, and half of Wall street ; with Mrs. Elizabeth Cady Stanton and Parker Pillsbury as editors, and Miss Susan B. Anthony as general manager and proprietor.

Let the one hundred thousand school teachers send in their subscriptions. We intend that two million dollars spent yearly in the perfumes to lay immortal wreaths on the monuments which in sweat and tears others have hewn and built; but for us . . . there is no name like the *Revolution*."

The motto on the *Revolution*'s masthead read: "Men, their rights and nothing more; women, their rights and nothing less." Anthony managed the office, handled the bookkeeping and bills, and hired the typesetters and printers, while Stanton served as senior editor and primary writer.

Although it lasted for only two and a half years, the weekly newspaper became a mouthpiece for some of the most prominent, creative, and uncompromising members of the women's rights movement. Matilda Joslyn Gage, Paulina Wright Davis, and Ernestine Rose—all highly dedicated and visionary leaders for women's rights— were regular correspondents. More important, the paper, under Stanton's direction, dealt with controversial issues that other papers and forums only touched upon gingerly. Abortion, regulation of prostitution, divorce, and prison reform—all were discussed openly in the *Revolution*'s pages as reasons why women needed political power.

Nor did the paper shrink from condemning the "degrading" legal position of married women and from disputing the traditional view of marriage as sacred and indissoluble. Stanton advocated more liberal divorce laws and better legal protection for married women and concluded that giving women the vote would help to rectify married women's legal inequities. The *Revolution* steadily focused the women's rights movement on the need for female suffrage, especially at a time when other reformers supported suffrage only for black men. The newspaper also linked female suffrage to dramatic and controversial reforms for women—reforms that more conservative factions of the movement were unwilling to raise.

The *Revolution* broke other new ground by reaching out to working-class women, whom the women's rights movement had previously ignored. Anthony, in particular, set out to capture working-class women's support. In September 1868, she helped to organize the Working Woman's Association "for the purpose of doing everything possible to elevate women, and raise the value of their labor." The *Revolution* reported on all proceedings of the Working Woman's Association, and Stanton and Anthony established a col-

An early militant feminist, Tennessee Claflin carried a banner in a New York demonstration by the International Association of Workingmen of the United States in December 1871.

umn entitled "The Working Woman" to highlight issues and events of concern to working-class women. They did not shy away from advocating policies that were highly unpopular, including equal pay for equal work and access to jobs traditionally reserved for men. Present-day working women are still struggling to achieve these goals. In acknowledging the problems of working-class women in the pages of the *Revolution*, Stanton and Anthony courageously laid the groundwork for more sustained political involvement by working-class women in later years.

Meanwhile, the conflict between those who supported women's immediate enfranchisement and those who chose to work for black male suffrage first and woman suffrage later on developed into a full-scale separation. By 1869, two organizations had emerged with differing visions and strategies. In May 1869, Stanton and Anthony founded the National Woman Suffrage Association (NWSA). This group refused to support the 15th Amendment—the amendment granting black male suffrage—unless it also enfranchised all women. NWSA members lobbied on a national level for a constitutional amendment to enfranchise women in all states.

In contrast, the American Woman Suffrage Association (AWSA), which was founded by Lucy Stone and Henry Blackwell in November 1869, supported passage of the 15th Amendment. Rather than seek a constitutional amendment to give women the ballot, members of AWSA appealed to individual state legislatures to pass state

Susan B. Anthony (center) and leaders of the National Woman Suffrage Association. NWSA advanced a daring vision of women's lives and dealt with such issues as wage inequities and stringent divorce laws, contraception, and abortion.

laws granting female enfranchisement.

Members of AWSA published their views in their own newspaper, the *Woman's Journal*. Like its parent organization, the *Woman's Journal* spoke to a more conservative and narrow vision of women's rights. It tried to cultivate the support of conservative middle-class readers by linking suffrage to middle-class benefits, such as higher education for women, professional advancement, and protection of married women's earnings and property from their husbands.

The *Woman's Journal* also avoided discussion of controversial issues, such as abortion and prostitution. It took a chattier, more compromising tone than the *Revolution* and focused strictly on suffrage news—debates, speeches, conventions, and political platforms favoring suffrage. Despite financial reverses and frequent staff changes, the *Woman's Journal* outlasted its rival, the *Revolution*, and eventually became the main organ of the women's rights movement. Lucy Stone was its chief editor, and former abolitionists William Lloyd Garrison, Henry Blackwell, T. H. Higginson, and Julia Ward Howe served as assistant editors.

For 20 years, the NWSA and AWSA pursued their separate goals, holding conventions, sponsoring debates, and sending speakers out on the lecture circuit. In 1887, Alice Stone Blackwell, daughter of Lucy Stone and Henry Blackwell, launched a campaign to merge the

Alice Stone Blackwell holds a copy of the Woman's Journal, *which was edited by her mother, Lucy Stone Blackwell. One reader observed that the paper could "corrupt you gradually." It featured such human interest columns as "Gossips and Gleanings," "Humorous," and "Concerning Women."*

two organizations. Three years later, in February 1890, the two as-sociations joined hands to become the National American Woman Suffrage Association (NAWSA). Elizabeth Cady Stanton served as the first president of NAWSA until 1892, when she withdrew from active involvement in organized suffrage efforts.

When Stanton died in 1902, the women's rights movement lost one of its most original and uncompromising voices. Anthony fol-lowed her into the presidency of the National American Woman Suffrage Association and remained at its helm until 1904. She died two years later. Although she was more cautious than Stanton in her thinking, Anthony was a courageous and tireless fighter for female equality.

American women had not yet received the constitutional right to vote, as Stanton and others had hoped for. But in the two decades between the rise of the National Woman Suffrage Association and the American Woman Suffrage Association in 1869 and their merger into the National American Woman Suffrage Association in 1890, the cause of female suffrage achieved important successes, especially in the western region of the country. The first victory for woman suffrage in the United States did not happen in one of the states of the Union. Instead, it occurred in the Wyoming Territory, a sparsely settled region with few political traditions in place. The conditions

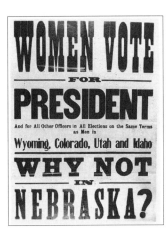

The women of Nebraska campaigned hard for the right to vote but did not receive it until the 19th Amendment to the Constitution was ratified on August 18, 1920.

of this region—the absence of long-standing political traditions and greater frontier opportunities for women—proved fertile ground for voting rights for women. In 1870, the tiny legislature in Wyoming passed a female enfranchisement bill, and the governor, John A. Campbell, who some years earlier had watched women conduct a women's rights convention in Salem, Oregon, signed it.

The neighboring territory of Utah followed suit in 1870. Most of Utah's settlers were Mormon. Although women held no important positions in the church hierarchy, they played an active role in community and church life. Church leaders encouraged women to serve as nurses and midwives, and some women even went to medical school. Mormon women also attended church meetings and voted on church matters, taught the younger children in their settlements,

In Cheyenne, Wyoming Territory, women line up to cast their ballots in the 1888 election. Women had won the vote there 18 years earlier.

raised money for the church, and educated themselves about government, history, and parliamentary law. The Mormon community's acceptance of women's public responsibilities no doubt contributed to winning female suffrage in Utah.

In the Northwest—the region now comprising Oregon and Washington—Abigail Scott Duniway, a brave and feisty woman, led the fight for woman suffrage. In 1852, at the age of 17, she journeyed with her family by wagon train to the Oregon Territory. There she married and raised five children and discovered firsthand what it meant to toil long hours for no wages: "To sew and cook, and wash and iron; to bake and clean and stew and fry; to be, in short, a general pioneer drudge, with never a penny of my own, was not pleasant business for an erstwhile school teacher," she wrote later. She also discovered that even though wives had no legal rights, a wife was responsible for any financial obligations undertaken by her husband. When Duniway's husband became disabled in an accident, she was forced to pay off his debts.

Abigail Scott Duniway led the woman suffrage fight in the Northwest. She believed that suffrage would give women greater control over their lives: "All we ask is to be allowed to decide, for ourselves, also as to what our rights should be."

By the age of 36, Duniway was ready to dedicate her life to woman suffrage. She established her own newspaper, the *New Northwest*, to convey her ideas and provide a forum for suffrage events out West. She also wrote and published vivid accounts of her travels throughout the Northwest. Duniway crisscrossed the region to give speeches and help organize suffrage events.

Duniway also clashed with East Coast suffrage leaders. She staunchly rejected their strategy of portraying women as morally superior to men in order to win public approval for female suffrage. She argued that this strategy perpetuated women's unequal political and economic status by sentimentalizing them. Instead, she urged, suffrage was the way to end the sexual and economic exploitation of women and give women a measure of control over their lives. Like Stanton, Abigail Scott Duniway was a clear-eyed, tough-minded, and dedicated suffrage leader whose unorthodox views did not always sit well with her more conservative suffrage sisters.

Southerners were even more resistant to women's rights. Because many early suffrage advocates had also been abolitionists, some Southerners regarded the movement as "a heresy that has a real devil in it," according to one suffrage worker traveling in Mississippi. Still, there were pockets of support for female suffrage throughout the South. Some Southern women joined the American Equal Rights Association, and in 1869 suffrage resolutions were offered at constitutional conventions in Texas and Arkansas, two former Confederate states applying for readmission into the Union. Although the resolutions did not pass, suffrage leaders were heartened that they had at least been introduced at such important events.

Southern women increasingly demanded their rights more forcefully. In 1871, a Virginia woman was turned away from the ballot box when she tried to vote. Unimpressed, she ceremoniously dropped a slip of paper into the box to assert her right to vote. But elsewhere in the former Confederacy, old "chivalrous" notions about gallant men and weak women died hard. "We do not need the ballot in Louisiana to protect any of our just rights and privileges," insisted one woman. "Every Southern woman has a protection and champion in every Southern man."

Although suffrage was the cornerstone of American women's campaign for political, social, and economic equality, it was not the only cause for which they fought. Suffrage fighters also envisioned ways to create more fulfilling lives for women. Antoinette Brown Blackwell, an ordained Congregational minister, author, wife, and mother, challenged the traditional notion that women's destiny lay in full-time homemaking. She praised the value of homemaking but urged women to seek employment outside of the home. "Women need a purpose," she declared, "a definite pursuit in which they are interested, if they expect to gather from it tone and vigor, either of mind or body."

Blackwell exhorted women to embark upon all endeavors—"industries, science, art, religion, and into the conduct and government of the State." But she did not want women to be overwhelmed by both household responsibilities and workplace obligations. Instead, she urged husbands to share housework and neighbors to share child care responsibilities. She suggested that workers share jobs, such as carpentry and blacksmithing, so they could experience greater variety in their daily lives. Blackwell not only envisioned social and political equality for women but also desired to bring about a more humane social order in which both men and women could lead joyous, productive lives.

Other crusaders for women's equality attacked the confining clothes

The Emancipation Waist.

MANUFACTURED BY

GEO. FROST & CO.

287 Devonshire Street, Boston.

Protected by Patents Aug. 3d and Sept. 7th, 1875.

Figure 1.

Figure 2.

THIS WAIST is universally acknowledged to be one of the best of the strictly hygienic Dress Reform garments. It is adapted for ladies and children, and when properly fitted to the form takes the weight of the outer clothing from the hips, doing away with skirt-supporters of all kinds, and distributing the strain over the shoulders.

BY THE PECULIAR cut and fit of the front, the breasts are supported and freed from compression, and also from the "drag" from the shoulders that many complain of who wear other Dress Reform garments.

THIS WAIST takes the place of the chemise, corset and corset-cover, and is so arranged that the bands of the outer skirts do not lay over one another, and although fitting the form closely, leave every nerve, vein and blood-vessel free to act, thus securing the recommendation and endorsement of all our leading physicians.

IT IS manufactured of fine white cotton cloth, with a lining of the same. As a ready-made garment we make it with the lacing on the side, as shown in Figure 1, above. Both plain and trimmed, (Figure 2) short and long sleeves.

6

The loose-trousered bloomers were designed to free women from the discomfort of binding corsets. Perhaps sensing the competition, the advertisement for the Emancipation Waist corset notes that the garment relieves the strain on women's bodies from supporting heavy skirts and permits good blood circulation.

that women wore. They believed that tight, heavy corsets and cumbersome bustles, which were fashionable throughout the 19th century, endangered women's health and restricted their freedom of movement. They urged women to dress for comfort and freedom rather than for fashion. Suggestions to reform women's attire had circulated within the women's rights movement as early as the 1850s.

Amelia Bloomer, editor of the women's rights journal *Lily*, was ridiculed for sporting loose-fitting harem pants, which quickly became known as bloomers. Elizabeth Cady Stanton also wore them for a time, as did other women. But the more comfortable attire created such a stir that Stanton and others stopped wearing bloomers in public for fear of diverting attention away from more urgent issues.

After the Civil War, women renewed their efforts to reform their clothing. In 1871, Tennessee C. Claflin, an outspoken and controversial advocate of women's rights, proclaimed dress reform to be "one of the most important Humanitarian movements of the age"—indeed, perhaps as important as the crusade for woman suffrage. She condemned current fashions for endangering women's health and that of the children they bore and for contributing to the image of women as sexual objects who dressed only for men's pleasure. Claflin urged women to cast off these life-threatening garments and dress for their own comfort, health, and pleasure.

Her sister, Victoria Woodhull, urged women to cast off not only confining clothing but also confining marriages. Woodhull was a proponent of free love, a movement that challenged the power and authority of organized religion and wanted to abolish the institution of marriage because it stifled true love.

Woodhull based her idea of free love on her view that the Constitution protected women's individual rights. Both women and men

At a convention in New York's Apollo Hall, Victoria Woodhull was nominated for President in 1872. She was backed by the National Woman Suffrage Association.

had the inalienable right to begin or end any intimate relationship, including marriage, because they were free and independent individuals. "I have an *inalienable, constitutional* and *natural* right to love whom I may . . . to *change* that love every *day* if I please," she declared.

Nevertheless, Woodhull's opinions caused the women's rights movement acute embarrassment because free lovers were lambasted in the popular press for their radical views. Woodhull herself earned the dubious title of "Mrs. Satan" and "Queen of Prostitutes." But the public's disapproval did not discourage her and Claflin from publishing *Woodhull & Claflin's Weekly*, the journal in which they espoused their controversial beliefs on free love, legalized prostitution, dress reform, and world government.

Woodhull was a fiery orator with a fiery message. In 1871, she addressed a meeting of the National Woman Suffrage Association, declaring, "We mean treason; we mean secession. . . . We are plotting revolution; we will . . . [overthrow] this bogus Republic and plant a government of righteousness in its stead." A year later, she made good on her words by running for President of the United States as a candidate of the newly organized Equal Rights party. Personal problems and scandals, along with the disapproval of her ideas among more conservative suffrage leaders, isolated Woodhull. She and her sister spent their last years in London, where Woodhull

The sisters Victoria Woodhull and Tennessee Claflin, who ran a stock brokerage in New York in the early 1870s, were satirized in this 1870 newspaper cartoon, entitled "The Bulls & Bears of Wall Street."

Spiritualism, the only religious movement to support women's rights, was highly popular among people who hoped to make contact with their dead loved ones.

continued to lecture and espouse controversial views. She was a brilliant, provocative woman who was far ahead of her time.

The late 19th-century women's rights movement included many such extraordinary and controversial fighters. Among the movement's most fascinating supporters were Spiritualists, mediums and other women who claimed to communicate with the spirit world. In their book *The History of Woman Suffrage*, Stanton and Anthony declared, "The only religious sect in the world . . . that has recognized the equality of women is the Spiritualists." Indeed, the Spiritualist movement began in the same year, 1848, and in the same region, upstate New York, in which the Seneca Falls convention for women's rights was held.

Spiritualism had great appeal. For those who claimed to have seen or communicated with the dead, Spiritualism assured them that the soul was immortal and that loved ones would be reunited in spirit after death. Moreover, followers of Spiritualism did not have to rely on a priest, minister, or other religious figure to explain the mysteries of death and the afterlife. They believed that they learned such truths from the spirits themselves through séances and other events in which they contacted the dead.

Spiritualism became a popular movement when two young girls, Kate and Margaret Fox, claimed to have made contact with the other side. Within months, other young women had also discovered a talent for contacting the spirit world, and séances were held in parlors throughout the North. Initially, adolescent girls were the most successful mediums, but later on older women also served as mediums.

Spiritualists, like members of organized religions such as Christianity and Judaism, claimed that women were pious by nature. But unlike organized religion, Spiritualism thrust women into visible leadership roles and supported the most progressive reform movements of the day. Spiritualists envisioned marriages in which women were equal partners, were able to control how many children they wanted, and were free to earn their own wages. Some advocated equal wages for equal work performed by men and women and called for more liberal divorce laws. Others urged women to reject corsets and other confining apparel and wear more comfortable clothes. And most Spiritualists advocated female enfranchisement.

In the 1870s and 1880s, Spiritualism provided some of the most effective speakers to promote female suffrage and other progressive ideas of the women's rights movement. Suffrage leaders in California relied greatly on Spiritualists and trance speakers in 1870 and dispatched three women mediums to present the first woman suffrage petition to the California state legislature. In Connecticut, New Jersey, Indiana, New York, and Michigan, mediums also played an active role in state suffrage campaigns. They were polished speakers who skillfully appealed to a moral authority higher than the power of the state; but they did so as moral guides themselves, not merely as vehicles for the spirits' ideas.

Despite the efforts of scores of individuals and suffrage groups, many years would pass before women won a constitutional amendment granting them the right to vote. In other respects, some women did achieve greater control over their lives, usually by becoming economically independent or by enjoying greater equality and autonomy within their marriages, an accomplishment that the Spiritualists and others championed. But, in general, women did not achieve many of the reforms that women's rights supporters called for.

One arena in which women did make significant strides, however, was in their ability to get a college education. Women had greater opportunity during the 25 years following the Civil War to pursue an education and, therefore, the pathway into economic independence and professional fulfillment than ever before. Between 1870 and 1900 the number of women college students throughout the country increased eightfold, from 11,000 in 1870 to 85,000 in 1900. In 1870, women constituted 21 percent of the college popula-

For a geology field trip at Smith College in the 1880s, the students sported stylish hats and brought along wicker picnic hampers.

tion. By 1900, they represented 35 percent. The postwar need for more teachers and for women who were able to step into positions left vacant by men lost in war contributed to this growing influx of female students. Moreover, women who had lost husbands or fiancés in the war now faced the daunting task of supporting themselves. To do that, they often needed more education. Other women, especially from middle-class families, simply thought that an education was their birthright.

Women could take two pathways toward a formal education. They could choose the less expensive teacher-training and business schools, or they could attend four-year colleges. Although coeducation for women and men became more acceptable by the 1870s, many parents preferred to send their daughters to all-female schools. After the war, newly established women's colleges thrived. In 1865, Vassar College in New York State was established. Ten years later,

Laboratory sciences were a part of the Smith curriculum from the college's earliest days. Entering students had to pass stringent examinations in mathematics.

in 1875, Smith College and Wellesley College, both in Massachusetts, welcomed their first classes. And in 1884, Bryn Mawr in Pennsylvania opened its doors. In the South, the Women's College of Baltimore, now Goucher, opened in 1884. Although professing to train women to be good "Christian" wives and mothers, these schools also offered young women a rigorous academic education in a supportive setting. Their creation was a critical milestone along the path of women's access to higher education.

The elite men's schools—Harvard, Yale, Princeton, and Columbia—still resisted admitting women. In 1874, Harvard faculty began to offer examinations but no instruction to women. A few years later, they instituted a comprehensive academic curriculum without granting degrees. Finally, in 1894, the Harvard Annex, as it was called, was chartered as Radcliffe College, with the power to grant academic degrees. Similarly, at Columbia, women took examinations from the college's professors, though they were not allowed to attend lectures. They protested, and Barnard College, the female affiliate of Columbia, opened in 1889. Other all-male colleges also established separate colleges for women to avoid admitting women into their schools.

In addition to the women's colleges, a few private and state uni-

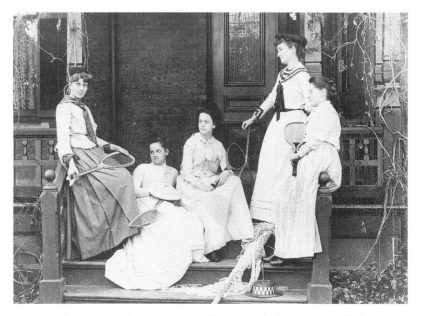

Though academic subjects were the focus of the women's colleges, they also provided recreational opportunities. Vassar fielded its first baseball team in 1876 (left), and Smith students (right) enjoyed tennis.

versities began to admit women. These included Boston University, a private college established in 1873 that was coeducational from the start, and several state universities. The University of Iowa had begun to admit women in 1855, and other state universities followed suit. The Universities of Kansas, Indiana, and Minnesota began admitting women in 1869, and state universities in Missouri, Michigan, and California followed a year later. Public universities in the South were more resistant, and many did not admit women until the early 20th century.

College administrators and educators put forth a variety of reasons to justify excluding women students. Among the most persuasive arguments in its time was the idea that a college education could damage a woman's ability to bear children. Dr. Edward Clarke, a retired Harvard Medical School professor, was a chief proponent of this theory. He argued that women needed to save their "limited energy" for childbearing. If they used it up by studying, they would, in his words, damage their "female apparatus." In 1873, he set forth his ideas in his widely read book, *Sex in Education*. But by 1885, a survey of coeducational institutions highlighted the positive effects of coeducation on both male and female students. Despite Clarke and his followers, higher education for women was here to stay.

American women would not gain the constitutional right to vote until 1920, when the 19th Amendment to the Constitution granted female enfranchisement. In 1890, this constitutional right was not yet in view. But women had asserted their claim to equal social and political rights and had organized a movement complete with competing organizations and strategies. In the process, they gained crucial political and organizational skills, and many women had found their life's work as speakers or writers for female suffrage and equality. By 1890, when the National Woman Suffrage Association and the American Woman Suffrage Association merged into the National American Woman Suffrage Association, there was no turning back to the days when women devoted their time to doing genteel good works, paid their taxes, or signed away their legal rights in marriage while silently bemoaning their lack of political power. As women waged the struggle to vote and to take greater control of their lives, they had other battles to fight as well—on the job, in their communities, and in defense of new visions of women's lives.

CHAPTER 3

"WOMEN HAVE ALWAYS WORKED":
NEW EMPLOYMENT OPPORTUNITIES

W hen the guns of battle were silenced at the end of the Civil War, another kind of roar could be heard from the mighty engines of industrial production as the reunited nation entered a period of unprecedented industrial growth. Iron, steel, textiles, lumber, meat packing, flour milling—these were just a few of the industries that mushroomed after the war. These businesses relied on new forms of mass production and, in the process, transformed the artisan, craftlike nature of many occupations into industries that relied on new technology and assembly lines, factories full of workers performing one task over and over.

In Paterson, New Jersey, for example, 4 silk mills employed 590 workers before the war. After the war, 10 more mills had sprung up, and 8,000 workers operated the mills. The one machine shop that had employed 10 workers before the Civil War employed 1,100 a few years later. And Paterson itself grew from a small town of 11,000 to a city of 33,000. Throughout the country, other towns and villages were undergoing equally rapid growth. Most of this growth took place in the North because the South was still recuperating from the devastation of war. Between 1860 to 1870, the total number of manufacturing companies in the North alone increased by 80 percent.

Owning their own businesses was something new for 19th-century women. Mrs. J. M. McDonough, shown here outside her upstate New York clothing store, was one such successful entrepreneur.

The expansion of the railroad system helped to knit the country together and enabled goods to travel from one area to another. On May 10, 1869, the finishing touches of a transcontinental railroad system were put in place. At Promontory Point, Utah, the Union Pacific Railroad, originating in Council Bluffs, Iowa, and the Central Pacific Railroad, whose starting point was in California, met as the last spike was nailed down. With this latest engineering feat, businesses were able to find newly accessible markets for their goods.

Although the poet Walt Whitman decried the "depravity of the business classes of our country" and Mark Twain, the renowned satirist, pronounced the country's political and commercial methods to be bankrupt, other public figures praised the nation's feverish rush to get rich. Throughout the 1870s and 1880s, a Baptist minister, Russell H. Conwell, traveled around the country preaching the gospel of wealth. "I say that you ought to get rich," he exhorted audiences. "It is all wrong to be poor."

Such sentiments encouraged a growing social and economic gulf

Bell Time, *drawn by Winslow Homer, illustrated the hard life of New England factory workers. The engraving was published in* Harper's Weekly *in 1868.*

between the rich and poor. With the emergence of big business came the concentration of great wealth in the hands of a very few. In 1884, a newspaper reporter described the grand setting of a banquet at Delmonico's, a fashionable New York restaurant: "The room was festooned with flowers in every direction. . . . And then the feast! All the dishes which ingenuity could invent or the history of past extravagance suggest were spread before the guests." In wide-eyed delight, the reporter went on to describe the costly wines served. Elsewhere in the nation, another New York paper reported that same year, 150,000 people were out of work, while another 150,000 earned less than 60 cents a day—many of them young women working 11 to 16 hours a day. During that year, 1884, 23,000 families were evicted from their homes because they were unable to pay the rent.

To be sure, the country's industrial growth had begun even before the war. And the war itself gave a giant boost to the nation's industrial life. Old factories were retooled and new ones were built to produce weapons, ammunition, machinery, clothing, ships, and canned goods. This expansion in industrial production provided new jobs for both men and women. During the war, women from the North, where most of the industrial production took place, found work in factories as replacements for men who had gone to war. They worked in textile factories, as clerks and copyists in government printing shops and offices, and as store clerks. Many women,

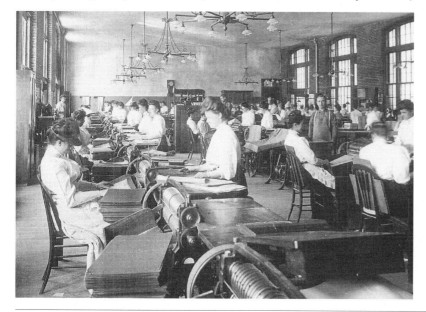

Urban women began to find work in offices. Women employees of the U.S. Treasury Department printed certificates for bonds that helped finance the Civil War.

North and South, became battlefield nurses, and some even disguised themselves as men and fought in the war.

During the following two decades, women continued to seek new forms of employment. They were forced, however, to protect themselves against efforts to give their jobs to returning soldiers or restrict them from entering new occupations. The postwar era was a time of opportunity for women seeking work. But along with the opportunities came new resistance to women as wage earners.

After the war, more young women worked and lived away from their families. Rural women, in particular, migrated to the country's urban industrial centers in search of work. Rural areas offered few ways to earn a livelihood, and opportunities to grow and experience the world seemed far more limited on the farm. Single young women migrated at a greater rate and earlier age than single men to seek work in the cities. On the average, single urban women were 18 years old while men were 20.

Although cities offered more employment opportunities, women's choice of occupations was limited primarily to jobs that men would not take or to work that seemed appropriate for women, according to the social standards of the day—that is, work that duplicated women's domestic and caretaking role, such as teaching, nursing, sewing, and domestic service. Women with few skills and little or

Sweatshops, so called for their poor working conditions and low wages, employed women of all ages. Women factory workers used many of the domestic skills they learned at home.

no education had even fewer choices. Factory work, waitressing, and domestic service were among their few available options.

Among these, many women preferred factory work because they perceived it to be less demeaning than housework. Yet factory work was arduous. Although most female factory workers were employed in the garment industry, women also worked in factories that made boxes, artificial flowers, canned foods, and other products. For all factory workers the hours were long—anywhere from 10 to 12 hours a day—and the loud clack-clack-clack of machines echoed in their ears as they sat hunched over their work for wages of less than a dollar a day. One female garment worker from Brooklyn, New York, told a magazine reporter: "The machines go like mad all day, because the faster you work the more money you get. Sometimes in my haste I get my finger caught and the needle goes right through it. . . . I bind the finger up with a piece of cotton and go on working."

In 1869, sewing women in New York City who worked at home were paid 4 cents for each pair of undershorts that they made. Although the sewing machine, which was invented in 1846, speeded up their work, they were still able to make only five pairs a day. This earned them 20 cents. On top of that, they had to pay for heat, light, and thread, reducing their final paychecks even more. At this time, the cheapest rooms in New York City cost about a dollar a

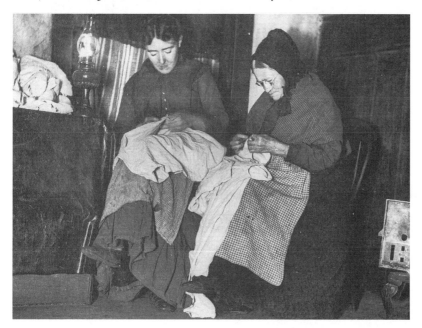

Women on the Lower East Side of New York City, a bustling but squalid immigrant community, often took in piecework. This photograph was taken by Jacob Riis, a social reformer who chronicled working-class life in New York.

Jacob Riis took this photograph of tenement families on Baxter Street, in New York City, in 1888. Though the apartments were overcrowded and unsanitary, such tenements provided a strong sense of community.

week. Once they paid their rent, they had only a few cents left over for food, clothing, medicine, and transportation. As a result, many single women shared rooms and beds with other working women. Even with this arrangement, they barely had enough money left for food. In 1869, one experienced seamstress declared, "I have worked from dawn to sundown, not stopping to get one mouthful of food, for twenty-five cents. I have lived on one cracker a day when I could not find work, travelling from place to place in pursuit of it."

Twenty years later, the standard of living for urban factory women was no better. In the late 1880s, the urban woman worker was paid an average of $5.58 a week, in contrast to $7.50 to $8.00 a week for a male worker. A woman's salary could drop to $5.24 if she had missed work because of illness or because she was laid off during a slow period at the factory. Yet the average cost of supporting herself in a city was about $5.51 a week.

Employers justified paying low wages to women by claiming that women were not supporting families and were working only for "pin money" to buy luxuries. But surveys of working women in the 1870s and 1880s found that most women who worked had no choice. Many supported themselves, and some contributed to family finances. In 1888, the United States Bureau of Labor reported that more than half of the working women surveyed, including women who lived at home, helped to support their families.

Besides the skills that a woman possessed, her class and ethnic background also influenced the work that she could find. Starting in 1880, a large influx of immigrants from eastern and southern Europe migrated to the United States. Most came from such countries as Russia, Poland, Bohemia, and Italy. They often joined friends and relatives who had immigrated earlier and found jobs in the factories where they worked. Like native-born American women, immigrant women chose factory work over domestic service because it felt less demeaning. Rose Cohen, a Jewish immigrant from Russia,

The artificial flower industry depended on the labor of entire families working in their homes. The pay was low and the hours were long.

This engraving, published in 1883 by the New York Bureau of Statistics of Labor, shows an extended family rolling cigars in a city tenement. Dinner awaits on the table at left.

recalled in her autobiography how disappointed her mother was when Rose took a job as a domestic. "Is that what I have come to America for, that my children should become servants?" her mother lamented.

Most Jewish and Italian immigrant women in large cities worked in the garment industry and in artificial flower-making. Polish and Slavic women worked in the textile mills of New England and the South or in meat-packing and food-processing plants in the Midwest. And women from Bohemia who were skilled cigar makers worked as cigar rollers in their new country. Irish and Scandinavian women in the North and African-American women in the South occupied the bulk of domestic service positions.

Most white domestic servants were young and single and lived with the families for whom they worked, usually in a small back or attic room. They earned from two to five dollars for a workweek that was even longer than the 60- to 70-hour workweek of most female factory workers. They usually had one afternoon off a week and had to be available to their employers the rest of the time. One young woman servant claimed that her employer would "sit in her sitting-room on the second floor and ring for me twenty times a day to do little things, and she wanted me up till eleven to answer the bell." To make matters worse, "I had no place but the kitchen to see my friends."

African-American women also chose domestic work as a last resort. To them, the relationship between employer and servant was painfully reminiscent of the relationship between mistress and slave. Most black women in Southern cities, however, could find no other work except for domestic service. But black domestics usually refused to live in their employers' homes and instead worked strictly as day servants. Cooks and maids earned between $4.00 to $8.00 a *month*, and nursemaids earned about $1.50 to $3.00. The workday generally lasted 12 to 14 hours, at least six days a week. Black women with children had to leave their own children with family or neighbors or all alone.

Although a black woman might be hired as a cook, she could also find herself watering the garden, cleaning house, or running errands. Her title may have specified a certain task, but her duties were as varied as her employer decided. Like white servants, she had to deal with impersonal and sometimes abusive behavior from her employer. She was variously called "cook," "girl," "Mammy," or by her first name, even by her employer's children.

In the South, mostly in Virginia, North and South Carolina, and parts of Kentucky and Tennessee, African-American women also worked in tobacco factories. Here, the worst jobs were reserved for them. These included sorting, stripping, stemming, and hanging the leaves—all tasks that required direct contact with the harsh tobacco leaves. Rehandlers, as workers who did this work were called, typically worked five and a half days a week for nine months of steady work. In 1880, tobacco workers in North Carolina earned 40 to 80 cents a day for a 12-hour day. They toiled under terrible conditions: The workrooms were dim and sweltering because sunlight and fresh air were shut out for fear of drying out the tobacco. In some factories, the fetid odor of an overflowing toilet filled the airless rooms.

Other black women took in laundry, and those who lived in coastal areas gathered and shucked oysters in factories. This work was as burdensome as tobacco stripping; shuckers stood at work benches all day and either steamed or pried the shells open to dislodge the precious oysters inside. Their weekly wages averaged between five and six dollars.

Until the 1910s, when thousands of African Americans migrated to Northern cities in search of work, most American blacks continued to live in the rural South, mostly in the former slave Cotton Belt

For Southern black women, domestic service was the most frequent occupation. Child care and cleaning were their prime responsibilities.

A white farm manager uses a primitive scale to weigh the cotton picked by black share-croppers. The proceeds of the crop were split between the pickers and the landowner.

states. There, African-American women shared with husbands, brothers, and fathers the hardscrabble life of sharecropping. For most black sharecropping families, a single misfortune, such as a flood, drought, fire, or illness, could bring financial ruin. Most families lived a stone's throw from starvation.

Throughout the last two decades of the 19th century, black sharecroppers continued to live and work at the mercy of the white landlord. He could force them to buy their farm implements and household supplies from him at inflated prices and could compel their children to work. William Pickens, the sixth of ten children in an Arkansas sharecropping family, recalled how their landlord in 1888 closed the neighborhood school to force the young people to work. "Very small children can be used to hoe and pick cotton," Pickens remembered, "and I have seen my older sisters drive a plow."

Besides helping out in the fields, the rural African-American woman often lent a helping hand to others—perhaps to a sister recuperating from a difficult pregnancy or to neighbors who needed her home-made herbal medicines. Her day usually began at four in the morning and ended long past midnight. Because she lacked the con-veniences that middle-class urban women increasingly enjoyed—such as running water, gas for heat and light, and ready-made clothing—she had to collect firewood and fetch water, prepare meals from scratch, and sew all of her family's clothing, on top of helping out in the fields about 12 hours a day. As one mother of nine later told an interviewer, "I worked many hours after they [her husband and chil-dren] was in bed. Plenty of times I've been to bed at three and four o'clock and get up at five, the first one in the morning."

When they were not toiling in the fields, African-American women

Sharecroppers supplemented their earnings by selling surplus produce at town markets. As in Africa, they carried their wares in baskets atop their heads.

In the tobacco warehouses of Virginia, black workers, both male and female, got the dirty job of picking and stemming the raw tobacco.

also took in laundry or sold homegrown produce or eggs from their hens. The saying "chickens for shoes" aptly described black women's desire to earn money from selling chickens and eggs to buy shoes for their children so they could attend school. Frances Ellen Watkins Harper observed that black mothers "are the levers which move in education. The men talk about it . . . but the women work most for it." They equated education with a better life and viewed their own toil as an investment in their children's future. Maude Lee Bryant, a sharecropping mother in Moncure, North Carolina, told an interviewer, "My main object of working was wanting the children to have a better way of living." She hoped that "the world might be just a little better because the Lord had me here for something, and I tried to make good out of it, that was my aim."

Parents seemed especially eager for their daughters to attend school. They knew that with an education their daughters could find work later on as teachers within the African-American community. From

1880 to 1915, more African-American girls than boys attended school, mainly because parents needed the labor of their sons in the fields. Even with an education, however, young black women had little hope of finding professional work outside the African-American community. Schools and businesses in the white community refused to hire them.

In contrast, white women with more education or the means to pay for business courses found new employment opportunities in office work. In 1870, there were only 19,000 female office workers nationwide; by 1890, this number had multiplied to 75,000. In 1870, only 4.5 percent of office stenographers and typists were women. Ten years later, women held 40 percent of these positions.

Although the workday was long—usually about 10 hours—the working conditions were more desirable and less hazardous than factory work, and salaries were relatively high. Moreover, the work was steady; unlike factory workers, office workers were seldom laid

Office work, formerly the exclusive domain of men, began to open to women, though they were still far outnumbered.

off during slow periods. In the 1870s, female office clerks who worked for the federal government could earn as much as $900 a year. Although women government workers earned less than men holding equivalent government positions, government jobs paid more than other professional work for women. A female teacher, for example, earned only $500 a year.

But some women had trouble finding jobs in offices. Most businesses refused to hire black women, and most were also reluctant to hire immigrant women. Some immigrant women changed their last names or disguised their parentage, place of birth, or address to pass themselves off as native-born American women.

Store clerking was another occupation that opened up to women. In 1870, 10,000 women worked as sales clerks. By 1890, that number had grown tenfold, to 100,000. Although the prospect of working in an elegant department store appealed to some women, the work was, in reality, very arduous and wages were low—about five or six dollars a week. On this meager salary, employees had to pay for room and board and purchase more expensive clothing suitable for work.

Saleswomen stood behind the counter for 12 or more hours a day. Until the 1890s, few stores permitted their saleswomen to sit down during business hours, and some clerks fainted from exhaustion. Like most companies that hired women to fill clerical and administrative positions, department stores hired no black women. Immigrant women who spoke fluent English without an accent were hired occasionally.

The post–Civil War era opened up new employment opportunities for women in nursing and teaching as well. Traditionally a job performed by women at home, nursing evolved into a profession after the Civil War, complete with professional training and accreditation. In 1873, Linda Richards became the first American woman to receive a degree in nursing. She graduated from Dr. Susan Dimock's nursing program at the New England Hospital for Women and Children in Boston, Massachusetts, and went on to teach at newly established nursing schools in New York, Boston, and Japan. She also founded several nursing programs. By the mid-1880s, 22 schools for nurses had opened in the United States.

African-American women had always ministered to their people's

This millinery shop in Passaic County, New Jersey, was staffed exclusively by women. It seemed only logical that women should sell fancy hats to each other.

medical needs. In slavery, they nursed sick or injured slaves and served as midwives and wet nurses to other enslaved women and to white mistresses. In freedom, they continued to care for ailing members of their communities, using herbs and potions in their treatments. But in the postwar era, they faced obstacles if they wanted to acquire a formal nursing education—most white nursing schools refused to admit black students. One exception was the New England Hospital for Women and Children, which admitted one black student and one Jewish student each year. In 1879, one of its students, Mary Eliza Mahoney, became the first African-American woman to receive a nursing degree.

By 1892, black women could choose from nursing programs at four black colleges: Spelman College in Atlanta, Georgia; Dixie in Hampton, Virginia; Provident in Chicago, Illinois; and Tuskegee

Teaching school has always been one of the most "acceptable" professions for educated women. This large but orderly class in Galena, Illinois, was taught by Miss Gardner.

Institute in Tuskegee, Alabama. The training was rigorous. At Spelman, for example, graduates took oral examinations before an audience of local citizens and dignitaries. Students were quizzed by faculty and visitors alike and had to demonstrate proficiency in bathing an infant, changing bed linen with a patient in the bed, and preparing and serving meals. These examinations served two purposes: Educators regarded them as an accurate measure of a student's nursing skills and knowledge and as a way to showcase their black students' intelligence and ability before skeptical visitors.

After graduation, most black nurses sought employment in private homes. Some went on to teach at other nursing and medical schools or joined the staffs of all-black hospitals. Black nurses also worked to improve public health within African-American communities, especially in the rural South. But nursing remained predominantly a white woman's occupation. In 1910, fewer than 3 percent of the trained nurses in the United States were black.

Besides nursing, teaching was the most acceptable profession for women. American women had taught since before the Civil War. But the enormous need to educate former slaves in the South, as well as to expand public schooling throughout the former Confederacy, created new opportunities for both Northern and Southern women to teach in the South. As immigrants flowed into the country during the 1880s and 1890s, Northern teachers also found plenty of opportunity to teach in the urban schools of the Northeast and Midwest. By the 1880s, two-thirds of the nation's public school teachers were women, and some women even moved up to the powerful position of school superintendent.

For African-American women in particular, imparting knowledge to a generation of black children who may have been born during slavery—when educating blacks was forbidden by many state constitutions—became a form of community service. Both Northern and Southern African-American teachers taught in segregated schools. They bravely coped with inadequate supplies, overcrowded classrooms, inferior buildings, and uncooperative white administrators—many of whom were deeply prejudiced.

But the rewards outmatched the drawbacks of such work. The children were eager to learn—in Richmond, Virginia, alone 96.5 percent of all black children attended school in 1890—and teachers were keenly aware of their responsibility to promote the advancement of their race. Fannie Jackson Coppin, a teacher and principal in Philadelphia, was fond of saying that "knowledge is power." To her, education was the bootstrap by which African Americans would pull themselves up the social and economic ladder. She tried to break down all employment barriers against blacks by urging students from even the most impoverished and illiterate families to aim high—to be doctors or lawyers, engineers or authors, or teachers for their own people. Writing to Frederick Douglass in 1877, Coppin passionately described the purpose of an education: "I need not tell you, Mr. Douglass, that this is my desire to see my race lifted out of the mire of ignorance, weakness and degradation: no longer to be the fog end of the American rabble; to sit in obscure corners in public places and devour the scraps of knowledge which his superiors fling him. . . . I want to see him crowned with strength

Elizabeth Blackwell (left) founded a medical college for women in New York City and established a rigorous course of study and clinical experience for her students. The Women's Medical College of Philadelphia (right), like Blackwell's college, included surgical training in its curriculum.

and dignity; adorned with the enduring grace of intellectual attainments."

Because the occupations of nursing and teaching were considered a natural extension of women's maternal and caretaking nature, women who wanted to go into these professions faced far fewer obstacles than women who wanted to become doctors or lawyers, two professions reserved almost strictly for men. A handful of women doctors had gone into practice before the war and paved the way for women's entry into the medical field. These included the diminutive but formidable Harriot K. Hunt, who taught herself medicine before attending lectures at Harvard University, and Elizabeth Blackwell, who was forced to go to Europe for her medical training. Along with her sister, Emily, she established the Woman's Medical College of the New York Infirmary for Women and Children.

By 1890, the University of Michigan had graduated 88 women doctors, the Woman's Medical College of the New York Infirmary had produced 135 women doctors, and the Women's College of Philadelphia had trained 560. In addition, hundreds of other women were beginning to enroll in medical school. Mary Putnam Jacobi, a doctor who taught at the Woman's Medical College in New York, explained why more women were entering the medical field: "Women have always worked," she observed. "But they demand now . . . a free choice in the kind of work, which, apart from the care of children, they may perform. The invasion of the medical profession is one of the more articulate forms of this demand." But hospitals balked at admitting female physicians to their staffs. As a result, the vast majority of female physicians went into private practice, where they continued to fight an uphill battle to attract patients, or joined the staffs of all-female hospitals.

If white women medical students and physicians faced resistance from a medical establishment rigidly dominated by men, then African-American women who aspired to be physicians encountered even more obstacles because of their skin color. But, undiscouraged, they forged ahead, establishing clinics and hospitals and serving the medical needs of their people. By 1890, 115 African-American women doctors were practicing in the United States.

Among these was Rebecca J. Cole, who graduated from the Female Medical College of Pennsylvania in 1867. She then worked with Elizabeth and Emily Blackwell at the New York Infirmary for Women and Children. Dr. Cole was a pioneer in practicing preventive medicine. She made house calls to tenement districts, where she taught basic hygiene and child care to women. She fought against overcrowded housing and became a formidable spokesperson for civil and economic rights for African Americans.

Like female physicians, women scientists and lawyers helped dismantle the barricades against women's professional advancement.

Dr. Rebecca Cole (standing, right) was one of the first black women in the United States to become a physician. Here, she attends a staff meeting at the New York Infirmary, where she was the chief sanitary inspector.

*In 1877, at age 59, astrono-
mer Maria Mitchell left the
climbing to a student at the
Vassar College observatory.
She received her earliest
astronomy training from her
father, who arranged for her
access to the Harvard College
observatory, but none of the
colleges that taught astronomy
in her day accepted women.
Mitchell discovered a comet
and became the first woman
elected to the American
Academy of Arts and Sciences.*

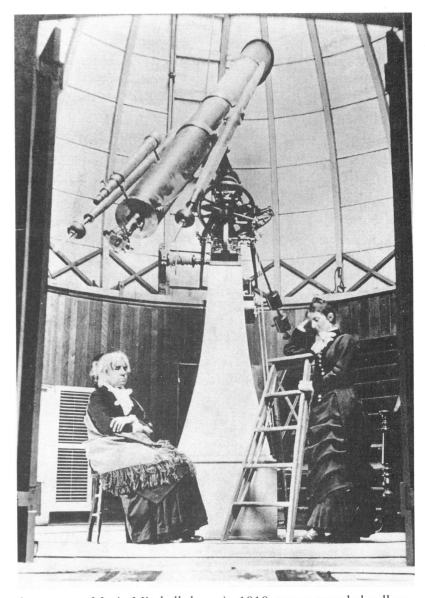

Astronomer Maria Mitchell, born in 1818, never attended college. Instead, her father taught her astronomy. When she discovered a comet in 1847, she gained international acclaim. In 1865 she joined the faculty at the newly established Vassar College, an all-women's college. Over the next several decades she trained other female astronomers, including her successor at Vassar, Mary Watson Whitney.

In the eyes of the male-dominated legal profession, women who sought to become lawyers were indeed scorning their "womanly duties." In 1869, Arabella Babb Mansfield petitioned the Iowa bar and became the first American woman to be licensed to practice law. She had taught herself law, a common practice before the turn of the century, and passed the Iowa bar examination. Mansfield encountered little hostility to her admission to her state bar.

But other women were not as lucky. Myra Bradwell of Chicago, organizer of her local chapter of the American Woman Suffrage Association and editor of a weekly legal journal, was refused admission to the Illinois bar because of her sex. She even appealed her case to the U.S. Supreme Court, but the Court also ruled against her. In 1872, however, while her case was still pending before the Supreme Court, the Illinois legislature passed a bill to admit women to the state bar, and she was admitted. Other similarly self-educated women challenged existing restrictions against admitting women to the bar and became lawyers. But until the late 1890s, most law schools still refused to admit women.

When Belva Lockwood applied to the law school at Columbian

This advertisement for a lecture by lawyer Belva Lockwood trumpeted her as "Queen of the American Bar" but also listed her more traditionally female accomplishments as "The Teacher and Lover of Children" and "The Untiring Friend of the Sick and the Poor."

The magazine Judge *poked fun at the temperance movement and at Belva Lockwood's run for President, portraying the campaigns as sideshows in a circus. Susan B. Anthony plays the cymbals, Elizabeth Cady Stanton the drums.*

College, later George Washington University, she was rejected because, according to the admissions committee, she would "distract the attention of the young men." She attended one of the few law schools that did admit women, National University Law School, and graduated in 1873, only to be denied the right to practice before two higher courts, the Court of Claims and the U.S. Supreme Court. Lockwood fought this discrimination and lobbied for a bill to allow any woman lawyer to appear before the Supreme Court after she had practiced in the highest courts of her own state or territory for at least three years. Congress passed the statute in 1879, and Lockwood became the first woman lawyer to argue before the Supreme Court.

Lockwood made news in other ways as well. In 1872, she supported the presidential campaign of women's rights advocate Victoria Woodhull, and in 1884 Lockwood herself was nominated as a presidential candidate by a group of women in California who had organized themselves as the National Equal Rights party. Her platform advocated equal civil rights for women, African Americans, and Native Americans; temperance (opposition to the consumption of alcoholic beverages); standardized marriage and divorce laws throughout the country; and universal peace. She received 4,149 votes in six states. After running for President again in 1888, she resumed practicing law.

Black law schools were not above practicing sexual discrimination either. In 1869, Mary Ann Shadd Cary, teacher and suffrage fighter, was the first woman to enroll in Howard University's law school. She studied law for two years but withdrew when the school denied her a law degree because of her sex. By 1872, however, the school had changed its policy, and Charlotte E. Ray, who graduated from Howard that year, became the first African-American woman lawyer. Cary returned to Howard many years later and received her Bachelor of Laws degree in 1883. She spent the rest of her life practicing law in Washington, D.C.

In other ways as well, women were making their voices heard. The postwar era was an extraordinarily rich one for women speakers, writers, and artists. Women such as American Red Cross founder Clara Barton and Frances Ellen Watkins Harper went on the lecture circuit to recount their wartime experiences or endorse female enfranchisement. Barton gave hundreds of speeches and usually charged $100 to $150, though she gave veterans' groups a discount. Scores of other women published autobiographies and memoirs about the war. Between 1865 and 1914, more than a hundred books and even more articles about women's wartime exploits were published.

New England poet Emily Dickinson avoided the public arena during her lifetime, but her poems—discovered after her death—are considered classics of American literature.

But women wrote about other subjects as well. Louisa May Alcott, born in 1832, is most well known for her moralistic novel *Little Women*, which was published in 1868 and became an instant success. In it, she glorified the traditional domestic ideal by portraying a cozy family of four sisters and their mother during the Civil War. Faith, love, and hope pull this family through difficult times. Alcott was a prolific writer who wrote several other novels for young readers and even tried her hand at some horror stories.

Emily Dickinson, born in 1830 in Amherst, Massachusetts, took inspiration from her beautiful surroundings for her lyrical nature poetry and her more brooding meditations in verse on love and life's impermanence. She penned more than 1,700 poems, but only two were published in her lifetime. As the years passed, she became ever more reclusive and avoided developing close friendships in person. Instead, she conducted a lively correspondence by mail and refined her poetic sensibilities. Her poems were her "letter to the world," as she declared in one verse. After her death in 1886, her sister discovered Emily's poems, neatly bound in packets in her dresser drawer, and pleaded with friends to have them published.

Ramona, a novel by Helen Hunt Jackson, focused on the lives of Native American women. "I did not write Ramona; it was written through me," Jackson later claimed. "My life-blood went into it—all I had thought, felt, and suffered for five years on the Indian question."

Authors Helen Hunt Jackson (1830–1885) and Sarah Orne Jewett (1849–1909) sought inspiration for their writings from their sense of connection with the land and the people who cultivated it. Like Emily Dickinson, Helen Hunt Jackson was born in Amherst, Massachusetts, but she lived for a few years in Colorado. There she learned firsthand about the injustices perpetrated against Native Americans. She confirmed her findings with further research in the New York Public Library. In 1881, she published a scathing indictment of government policy toward Indian tribes, entitled *A Century of Dishonor*. At her own expense, she sent copies to numerous government officials and every member of Congress.

She undertook other fact-finding projects on behalf of Native Americans, then changed her creative focus to fiction. In 1884, she published *Ramona*, a historical novel about a Native-American woman in California. Though simplistic and sentimental, the novel focused public attention on the injustices borne by Native Americans.

Sarah Orne Jewett, chronicler of rural life in Maine, celebrated the quiet virtue and dignity of rural people. Jewett tried to capture the texture of unremarkable, deeply rooted lives in fictional sketches and such novels as *Deephaven* (1877) and *The Country of the Pointed Firs* (1896). Her stories celebrated the land and captured a sense of place, illuminating as well the character of the people who lived there. Looking back, she described what she was trying to achieve in her writing: "I determined to teach the world that country people were not the awkward, ignorant set those persons seemed to think.

I wanted the world to know their grand, simple lives."

Women created in other ways as well. Edmonia Lewis, born in 1845 to an African-American father and Chippewa Indian mother, became a renowned sculptor in the 1860s and 1870s. Many of her works celebrated the emancipation of American slaves. Her sculpture *Hagar in the Wilderness*, completed in 1868, was a dramatic depiction of the biblical female slave. She felt moved to undertake this work out of a "strong sympathy for all women who have struggled and suffered," as she put it. At the Centennial Exposition of 1876 in Philadelphia, which commemorated the 100th anniversary of the Declaration of Independence, six of Lewis's sculptures were put on display.

Lilla Cabot Perry (1848–1933) and Mary Cassatt (1844–1926) both studied painting in France and were among the few women artists associated with Impressionism, the great French movement in art. This movement rejected the tendency in art to literally reproduce a scene in paint, as if the artist were trying to create the effect of a photograph. Instead, Impressionist painters approached their art from a very subjective, or impressionistic, response. Rather than convey a detailed and accurate rendering of the subject matter, they played with color and light to create a more free-flowing, vibrant, and atmospheric effect. Their subjects ranged from busy downtown Parisian streets to tranquil country farms and meadows.

Cassatt was the first American artist to show her work in an Impressionist exhibition. But unlike many other Impressionists, she chose to depict women and children in her work. Her paintings portray gentle, loving moments between women and their young children. Both she and Perry knew the great master of French Impressionism, Claude Monet, and their paintings reveal the Impressionist's broad brush strokes, brilliant use of color and shading, and desire to paint the fleeting moment.

Despite their talent, however, Cassatt, Perry, and other women artists faced many obstacles in gaining acceptance in a male-dominated vocation. More ornamental arts, such as painting china, were among the few socially approved ways for women to express their artistic talents. Women who wanted to be serious artists seldom had the financial resources and encouragement to achieve their goals. Many art schools would not admit women students. During these closing

Hagar in the Wilderness *by Edmonia Lewis. Lewis gave voice in her sculpture to the suffering of the oppressed, and she developed an international reputation.*

years of the 19th century, Mary Cassatt, Lilla Cabot Perry, and Edmonia Lewis were among the few women artists and sculptors to achieve their creative potential.

Women also tried their hand at inventing. American women had invented labor-saving devices since the early 19th century. But an outpouring of women's inventions, especially those that made domestic chores such as cooking, cleaning, and sewing easier, occurred in the postwar era. After four long years of war, with its discomforts and deprivations, women were eager to restore order and convenience to the domestic realm. Advances in tools, materials, and machinery enabled inventors to tinker with new possibilities for labor-saving devices.

In 1867, Margaret Knight of Massachusetts introduced a machine that made more durable paper bags. Helena Augusta Blanchard invented the first sewing machine that could sew complicated zigzag seams, and in 1873 Amanda Theodosia Jones developed a method for canning and preserving fruit without first having to cook it. Other women devised undergarments made without bone or wire to allow women to move around more easily. Women inventors had a variety of motives for introducing their inventions. Some were shrewd businesswomen who realized their ingenuity could make money for them. Others, especially inventors of less confining corsets, hoped their inventions would enhance the quality of women's lives. They

Margaret E. Knight received a U.S. patent for this paper bag-making machine in 1879. Knight, who later said that as a child the only toys she ever wanted were a "jackknife, a gimlet and pieces of wood," also invented a shoe-cutting machine and a window frame and sash, among other devices.

expressed a feminist desire to give women more freedom of movement and control over their lives—in this case, through less restrictive and more comfortable clothing. Women inventors demonstrated that women's creative and inventive abilities knew no bounds, and they proved that women were equally at home standing over a cookstove or drafting a blueprint of a new mechanical device.

"Women have always worked," declared Dr. Mary Putnam Jacobi. And indeed they have, but in the aftermath of the Civil War and during the nation's inexorable march toward industrial growth, women found growing opportunities to earn a living. However, the new factories and stores that employed women paid them low wages for long hours and often hazardous work. Women who fought to get an education and have a career faced many barriers if they wanted to be doctors or lawyers instead of nurses and teachers. African-American and immigrant women faced even more obstacles because of their race and ethnic origin. America was not ready to grant women all of the opportunities for gainful employment and professional advancement that men enjoyed. Many women and men still viewed the occupation of mother and wife as women's chief role in life. And only when women argued that their work was an extension of their maternal role did they gain professional acceptance by male peers. The quest for professional advancement and for equal pay for equal work swept postwar American women into the 20th century—and continues to this day.

CHAPTER 4

"I WISH I HAD MANY HANDS": TOILERS ON THE LAND

Although the nation rapidly developed into an industrial power in the years after the Civil War and many young men and women migrated to the cities to work in new factories, other women and men continued to live in rural areas. Some people even left the cities to seek a better life in the still undeveloped western region of the United States. In 1860, almost half the entire area of the United States was settled only sparsely. This region extended from the western border of Missouri to the shores of California and from the U.S.–Canadian border all the way south to lower Texas.

Several states in this territory had already been admitted into the Union. These included California, which was admitted in 1850, and Texas, which entered in 1845. As their populations soared, other territories also became states. In 1867, Nebraska entered the Union, and Colorado followed in 1876. North Dakota, South Dakota, Montana, and Washington all entered in 1889, and Idaho and Wyoming were both admitted the following year.

But this region had been populated long before it was carved up into states. Hispanic peoples had moved up north from Mexico into Texas and then pushed up into California and New Mexico. Native Americans had long called the western lands their home. The Sioux, the biggest and most powerful of the western tribes, inhabited the

The yoke of water buckets borne by this Arizona pioneer is an apt symbol of the hard work contributed by women to the building of the American West.

Sacramento, California, in 1849 was merely a tent town, as the California gold rush attracted Easterners who hoped to strike it rich.

woodlands of Minnesota and the Great Plains, and the Cheyennes dwelled in the region of the Powder River and Bighorn country of Wyoming and Montana. Farther south, other Cheyenne tribes established villages on the Colorado and Kansas plains. The Apaches occupied the arid southwest region of Texas and New Mexico; the Pueblos also lived in New Mexico. The Nez Percés claimed the Blue Mountains of Oregon and the Bitterroot Range of the Rocky Mountains between Idaho and Montana as their homeland. Many smaller tribes also inhabited the western lands.

For centuries, until the first non-Indian settlers started trickling into this region, Native American peoples coexisted, not always peacefully, farming the land, relying on the great herds of buffalo for meat, clothing, and shelter. Starting in the 1840s, the trickle of settlers onto the lands of Native Americans and Hispanics turned into a steady stream. The California gold rush of 1849 brought the first flood of migrants from the East Coast and Europe. Other settlers came in search of more fertile farmland and grasslands for their cattle and sheep to graze on. On the Texas Panhandle and the plains of Kansas, Nebraska, and North and South Dakota, they built farms and ranches and set their livestock free to roam and graze on open land. The populations of all of these areas surged. During the 1870s and 1880s, for example, the population of the predominantly farm states of Minnesota, Kansas, Nebraska, the Dakotas, Colorado, and Montana soared from one million to about five million— eight times the rate of increase of the country as a whole.

By 1890, the flow of migration out west had begun to wane.

The buffalo—the main staple of Native Americans—had been wiped out by thoughtless sportsmen, and Native American tribes had endured many bloody clashes with the U.S. military. Driven from their ancestral homes by settlers eager to lay claim to their land, they were forced to resettle on reservations. These were designated patches of land that hardly sustained their physical and spiritual needs. Their former lands were overtaken by settlements ranging from primitive outposts to thriving cattle towns. For women of all ethnic backgrounds—Native American, Hispanic, white, and African-American—who were part of the mosaic of western settlement, the feverish activity of these years had a profound impact upon their lives.

Although customs and practices varied among tribes, Native American women enjoyed greater social equality with Native American men than white women experienced in their own culture. Beyond their childbearing capabilities, Native American women performed essential tasks in their tribes. While the men hunted game, women collected seeds and roots and harvested crops. In fact, about five thousand years ago in Mexico Indian women may have been the first to domesticate corn.

Native American women worked together to plant, harvest, and grind the corn. As an old woman, Buffalo Bird Woman of the Hidatsa tribe of North Dakota vividly recalled how the women of her family planted corn together in the late 19th century. "I liked to go with

Protected from the hot New Mexico sun, Piute women gather seeds in woven baskets. Their contributions were essential to their families' livelihoods. This photograph was taken by John K. Hillers, the official photographer of the U.S. Geological Survey in the 1870s and 1880s.

my mothers to the cornfields in planting time, when the spring sun was shining and the birds singing in the tree tops," she remembered. "We cared for our corn in those days, as we would care for a child; for we Indian people loved our fields as mothers love their children." In winter, especially when game was less plentiful, the corn that Native American women harvested, along with seeds and roots that they gathered, sustained their tribes.

Because of their important food-gathering responsibilities, women played both a crucial spiritual and economic role in their tribes. Indeed, the social life of the tribe often revolved around matrilineal clan groups. Under this matrilineal arrangement, people divided themselves into kinship groups, in which groups of related women, their husbands, and their children lived together. A family's ancestry was traced through the female line, and children belonged to the mother's clan group.

This arrangement did not give Indian women special power over Indian men. Instead, it indicated that women were valued and influential members of their tribes. Though few women chiefs and warriors were to be found, Native American women served their people in equally important ways—as tillers of the land. Women worked together to carry out other tasks as well. They shared responsibility

James Mooney, an ethnologist with the Smithsonian Institution, photographed these Hopi women at work. The married woman, at left, grinds corn; the single woman is baking breads. Their marital status is indicated by their hairstyles.

Wichita women construct a grass lodge in Omaha, Nebraska. In many tribes, women had the responsibility of home building, though the materials and specific skills they used varied from place to place.

for child care and for constructing the basic building materials for the tribe's shelter. Pueblo women of the Southwest built the adobe walls of large, multiunit dwellings, and in the Northeast, Native American women wove mats out of reeds to drape over wood frames.

As settlers advanced farther west, Native American women found their important tribal roles gradually changing and disappearing, especially as their tribes lost control of their lands. Up until 1867, the U.S. government maintained treaties with Native American tribes. These treaties specified which regions remained under tribal control and which were open to settlement by other people. But after 1867, Congress abolished the treaty system and devised a reservation plan by which Native Americans were forced to leave their native lands— usually under armed escort by the U.S. military—and relocate in smaller areas reserved for them.

Sarah Winnemucca, a Piute Indian from Nevada, witnessed the forced resettlement of her people in 1878 from their Nevada home-land to the Yakima Indian reservation in eastern Washington. They had only three days to prepare for the treacherous journey over snow-bound mountains in the middle of winter. They traveled by wagon and camped out at night in frigid weather. Upon reaching the reser-vation, the tribe discovered that their new lodgings were wholly in-adequate. They were crowded into a makeshift shed and did not have enough clothing or fuel among themselves to keep warm. "Oh,

Sarah Winnemucca, from a Piute tribe in Nevada, emerged as a fearless spokeswoman for Native American rights. She embarked on lecture tours, protested to government officials, and wrote Life Among the Piutes *to publicize her cause.*

how we did suffer with cold," Sarah Winnemucca remembered. "There was no wood, and the snow was waist-deep, and many died off just as cattle or horses do after travelling so long in the cold." Sarah Winnemucca recorded her experiences and the sufferings of her people in her book *Life Among the Piutes: Their Wrongs and Claims* (1883). She also traveled to Washington, D.C., in the early 1880s to protest government policies toward Native Americans, and she lectured around the country.

Her startling facts aroused public sympathy, but the government did not change its policies. Indeed, its callous disregard for the rights of Native Americans came to a head at the massacre of Wounded Knee in 1890. After capturing a band of Sioux near Pine Ridge, South Dakota, a contingent of U.S. cavalry marched the group of 350 men, women, and children to a camp near a creek called Wounded Knee. There, they attempted to disarm the Indians of all their weapons. In the process, a gun owned by one of the Indians went off. Some witnesses said that the Indian fired it; others maintained that it went off when soldiers tussled with the Indian as he tried to put it down. The true answer remains unknown. The soldiers immediately opened fire and within minutes 153 Indian men, women, and children were dead. "We tried to run," Louise Weasel Bear remembered, "but they shot us like we were a buffalo."

In the last decades of the 19th century, Native Americans continued to be herded off their lands and forced into reservations. There, both men and women tried to maintain their intimate and cooperative relationship with the land, but reservation officials discouraged them from establishing cooperative farms and instead encouraged them to farm individual plots. As a result, Native American women gradually lost control of the land, and their social power within their tribes diminished. The equal relationship between Indian women and men changed and began to resemble the marital relations of the white settlers, in which a husband held economic and social power over his wife.

As their way of life eroded, both Native American women and men were forced to enter into a servile relationship with white settlers. Indian women, and some men, washed clothes and dishes and did other household chores for settlers. Some Indian women worked as nursemaids for white women. As their lands were scooped up by

non-Indians eager to wrest a profit from the land, Native Americans' communal, agrarian way of life vanished—and with it, the Native American woman's prominent tribal role.

Hispanic peoples suffered a similar displacement from their land and culture. From the 16th century onward, Spanish conquerors and explorers in Mexico married into Native American cultures. The offspring of these marriages became the Hispanics, who migrated up north over the centuries from Mexico to settle in the arid deserts of the American Southwest, the region comprising what is now New Mexico, Arizona, Texas, and Colorado.

Like Native Americans, Hispanics lived and worked cooperatively and relied on the land for their livelihood. In most villages, each family owned a small lot, a house, and the land immediately surrounding the house. The remaining land, along with all water rights, were owned by the villagers together. In this way, a system of private property coexisted with shared property. Villagers pooled

Jacinta Serrano, a basket maker at the San Gabriel Mission in California, found a ready market among white tourists. Hispanics and Native Americans living in Catholic missions and on government reservations tried to adapt traditional crafts to the commerce of the whites.

labor as well as natural resources. Women worked together to plaster houses, bake bread, spin wool, and stuff mattresses. Men also shared tasks, such as plowing, hoeing, harvesting, and caring for livestock. Sometimes families bartered goods; for example, one family might exchange wool for foodstuff.

Farming tasks were also divided between women and men. Men chose the crops for communal fields, and each wife took exclusive control of the family's garden plot, which produced most of the family's food. When men were away, women also took charge of the village's communal fields. Like Native American women, Hispanic women contributed significantly to their villages' sustenance. One indication of women's important village role can be seen in inheritance practices; unlike Anglo inheritance practices, which favored sons over daughters in dividing up an estate, Hispanic daughters and sons inherited wealth equally. Sometimes, however, daughters inherited

Hispanic women in Abiquiu, New Mexico, plaster an adobe building. Women worked cooperatively at many tasks.

livestock, furniture, and household goods instead of land. Among the villagers themselves, there were few differences in economic status. Wealthier families lived apart and rarely mingled with their neighbors of more modest means.

In the 1870s, Hispanic villages remained almost untouched by the growing presence of white, or Anglo, settlers. Some Hispanic men performed seasonal work for Anglo settlers for extra cash, then returned to their villages. This extra income enabled Hispanic farmers to purchase additional livestock or open a store.

By the 1880s, however, an expanding railroad system brought more white settlers to the Southwest. As more Anglos arrived, they forced their cultural values and business practices on Hispanics. They imposed the notion of private property, the use of property for commercial gain rather than for subsistence, and an economy based on money instead of barter. Most important, they simply took land that had been commonly owned by Hispanic villagers. Lacking sufficient pastureland, villagers could hardly sustain their agrarian way of life on their small individual plots. Gradually, Anglos gained control over the local village economy throughout New Mexico, Arizona, and Colorado. With insufficient land to support themselves, Hispanics had no choice but to work for the new landowners.

Hispanic women were no longer able to help support their communal life. They began to work for whites as seamstresses, cooks, launderers, domestics, hotel keepers, and even prostitutes. Like Native American women, they worked as day laborers for someone else instead of as farmers for their own people. They had no control of the hours or terms of their work, and they lost their important role in their own communities as food-producers. Gradually, Native American and Hispanic women had to relinquish a life rooted to the land for one based on wage labor.

In contrast, white and black women homesteaders heading west faced a life very much dependent upon the bounty of the land. Men and women went west for a variety of reasons—for the adventure, for a fresh start in life, to follow friends or family members who had preceded them, and mostly to seek a better livelihood. Southerners recovering from the wartime devastation of their economy saw in the West an opportunity to regain the wealth that they had lost in the war.

Mexican-American laundresses in Arizona worked for their white neighbors, earning cash they could bring back to their own communities. Many Mexican Americans started their own businesses.

Settlers received plenty of encouragement for these hopes. In Colorado and New Mexico, promoters advertised in pamphlets "Where to Go to Become Rich." The governor of New Mexico boasted about the enormous reserves of gold, silver, and copper to lure settlers to his region. For people barely scratching out a living, such grandiose promises of instant wealth were irresistible. Promoters also assured settlers that the clear, dry climate of the West would bring instant good health.

White native-born women made up the bulk of women journeying west. African-American women also made the arduous journey but in far fewer numbers. From 1878 to 1880, however, hundreds of African-American women headed for Kansas along with their men. There, they hoped to find greater economic opportunity and freedom from racial prejudice. Some even emigrated in organized groups. By 1880, 15,000 black migrants in Kansas were trying to scratch out a living as farmers and laborers. Called Exodusters, they built huts made out of sod bricks and planted wheat. Some organized self-sufficient colonies or worked for white settlers as farm laborers or servants.

For most Exodusters, Kansas proved to be no refuge, and some moved on to Nebraska and Oklahoma or returned to the South. Luckier migrants managed to stay and make homes for themselves.

Willianna Hickman, an Exoduster who migrated to Kansas from Kentucky in 1878, recalled that she cried from despair when she saw her new community, a collection of dugouts built against sloping dirt. But the "days, weeks, months, and years passed and I became reconciled to my home. We improved the farm and lived there nearly twenty years." The Exodusters, however, were a tiny minority. Most African Americans could not afford the journey out west and remained in the cities and rural hamlets of the South.

Both single and married women made the journey west. Some married women went reluctantly, knowing they had little choice but to follow their husbands. Others eagerly shared their husbands' dreams of a new life on a new land. Still others stayed behind while their husbands went ahead, waiting and wondering what their new homes would look like. Maggie Brown of Virginia waited a year and a half before joining her husband, Charles, in Colorado. During that time, she feared that he was becoming immoral and unfaithful to her. Nothing Charles wrote in his letters could reassure her until she joined him and saw for herself that Charles had remained faithful.

The trip out west was very hard. Travelers relied on several kinds

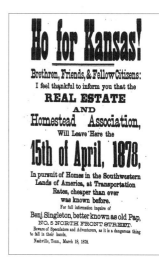

After Reconstruction, Southern blacks, later called Exodusters, headed north to Kansas in search of a better life.

of transportation: train, stagecoach, wagon, or ship. Traveling by ship was faster, but most travelers chose to go by land because that was less expensive. If they brought livestock with them, they walked most of the way to shepherd their animals along. Although men mostly handled this task, women also took their turn on foot, prodding their cattle or oxen along, while the men drove the wagons that held their belongings.

On the journey, women who traveled as part of a wagon train often carried out the same responsibilities that they did back home— cooking, washing, and caring for children. But they did so under much more primitive conditions. They had to contend with constant dust and cramped quarters. For some, their first big test of withstanding the frontier came when they had to collect dried buffalo dung, which was used as fuel. Some women could not bring themselves to touch the dried droppings, but they had no choice if they wanted to make a fire for heating water or cooking.

Women cooked under crude conditions, with few ingredients.

A wagon train poses for a portrait as it travels through Colorado. When families traveled together, women forged firm friendships that sustained them on the journey.

They supplemented staple diets of beans, bread, and bacon with wild berries gathered along the way, and occasionally served a few luxury dishes, such as canned oysters or eggs that had been carefully packed. They also added game and fish caught nearby.

Women shared household responsibilities along the way and welcomed one another's companionship. At night, around the campfire or at crude inns where travelers stayed, women eagerly visited together, knitting, crocheting, or merely resting their tired feet. They confided in each other, sharing thoughts they were perhaps reluctant to admit to their husbands. Annie Green, a homesteader from Pennsylvania, struck up an acquaintance with a "very dear lady" who was also heading out to Colorado. "We spoke to each other of our future prospects, mingled with hopes and fears," Green later recalled. But five weeks after they had all arrived, her friend died of pneumonia.

Such were the uncertainties of women and men who went west. Friendships made along the way abruptly ended when fellow travelers died or went their separate way. The ever-present threat of illness and the fear of attacks by Indians haunted travelers. The eerie howl of wolves at night, the fear of poisonous snakes and prowling bears, the relentless desert sun beating down, and the bitter cold nights up in the mountains—all of these fears and hardships tormented travelers. Even the desolation of the landscape itself seemed threatening. Riding through South Dakota's Black Hills, Annie Tallent recalled, "I could not help glancing furtively from side to side of the ravines to see whether there were any gnomes or hobgoblins peering out at us from between the crevices of the great rocks."

Women's responses to the landscape and especially to their new homes out west varied widely. Of her new surroundings in Colorado, Annie Green wrote, "Not a tree, plant nor shrub on which to rest my weary eye, to break the monotony of the sand beds and cactus of the Great American Desert." In contrast, Mary Ronan, who lived on an Indian reservation in western Montana in the late 1870s, loved the surrounding countryside, especially the tangy fragrance of June roses and the colorful patches of blue lupine. When she saw her new homeland for the first time, she was enchanted: "So beautiful the valley was that it seemed to me I had entered a place like the Garden of Paradise."

On the desolate Kansas prairie, a pioneer woman gathers chips of buffalo dung for fuel. Some women could not bring themselves to touch the dried droppings, but they had no choice if they wanted to make a fire for heating water or cooking.

Still, the hardships of the journey itself often paled in comparison to the hardship of setting up a home in a wilderness land. Depending on where they settled, a family's lodgings varied dramatically. In the deserts of New Mexico and Arizona, "home" might be a log cabin with dirt floors or a tiny cottage made out of adobe (a mixture of clay and dirt). In Kansas, many settlers lived in soddies, dwellings dug out of hard-packed soil. These makeshift dirt homes leaked or even dissolved in rainstorms, and snakes, worms, and centipedes made their homes in the walls and dirt ceilings of these dwellings. Many a pioneer woman awoke in the morning to discover she was sharing her bed with a snake that had fallen from the ceiling the night before.

Other families lived in tents or in their wagons until they could build a suitable shelter for themselves. Annie Green of Colorado recalled, "After securing several lots in the new town, we pitched our tent, which was almost daily blown to the ground. To say that I was homesick, discouraged, and lonely, is but a faint description of my feelings." Malinda Harris, a black Exoduster in Kansas, actively discouraged others from coming to Kansas. She wrote in a letter: "dont study a Bout coming away. if I knowed what I know no Body could not Pull me a way [from her former home]. . . . Pray for me for I kneed [sic] Prayers."

But women made do. They tried to make their homes as cheerful as possible by tacking up brightly colored pieces of cloth, by whitewashing the walls or covering them with canvas muslin or even newspaper, and by hanging up pictures. Treasured possessions brought

The dugout of the Mead family near Bloom, Kansas, housed several generations. Its single room, chock-full of furniture and cooking equipment, was a study in contrasts, containing a primitive washtub alongside an ornate stove and good china. Women did their best to make these damp, dirty hillside dwellings as homelike as possible.

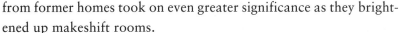

Child care, cooking, and laundry were mainstays of women's lives on the Kansas frontier. Washing equipment was primitive—brushes, washboards, and tubs—and the soap was homemade.

from former homes took on even greater significance as they brightened up makeshift rooms.

Most women who went west believed that their main responsibilities revolved around homemaking—taking care of husbands and children. Back home, such beliefs had perhaps limited their choices by discouraging them from doing work that was not deemed appropriate for women. But in their new homes, these beliefs provided a sense of stability that offset how uprooted they felt from familiar surroundings and family and friends. Cooking, cleaning, sewing the family's clothing—these tasks reassuringly linked them to the routine of earlier and easier times. And, as they did along the journey, women shared their chores with other women if possible, visiting as they washed clothes in a nearby creek or baked bread together.

Women, then, understandably took pride in making a home under difficult circumstances—a well-baked pie or well-made shirt were true accomplishments. These homemaking activities were also potential sources of income. Annie Green baked and sold bread. Not only did she earn four dollars in profit but, she claimed, she had "gained the reputation of giving larger loaves than any other person engaged in the business in town." She regarded her labors as both a right and an extension of her domestic responsibilities; to her way of thinking, her earnings helped improve her family's standard of living. Women settlers believed that their obligation to create a healthy and stable home life justified their desire to earn money for their families' benefit.

Their domestic sense of responsibility also justified their desire to build institutions and create organizations that improved their communities. Sunday schools, prayer meetings, church socials, reading clubs, debating societies, amateur musical and dramatic groups, and libraries—women took the lead in organizing these groups and institutions because they desired to bring culture, stability, and morality to an untamed land, especially for their children's benefit. Within a year after settling Kansas, women had organized charitable societies and a local chapter of the Woman's Christian Temperance Union, the national organization dedicated to outlawing the consumption of alcohol.

By establishing such institutions, women were quietly challenging the values of a social and political order dominated by men. They celebrated the way in which they were different from men. Men were physically strong and could do the physical work of building

Temperance crusaders pray in front of an Ohio saloon in 1873. Such scenes were commonplace as women worked to improve the temper of society, but the saloons' customers sometimes reacted by pouring beer on the women from the upstairs windows.

homes and schools. But women perceived themselves to be morally and spiritually strong; their vision and guidance created the schools built by men, and it also obligated them to rid their frontier communities of such undesirable practices as excessive drinking, gambling, and prostitution. Just as urban women used the values that defined the ideal domestic realm—purity, piety, moral goodness—to justify their volunteer activities in their communities, so women settlers drew on these very values to establish social order on the frontier. As wives and mothers, or simply as women, they felt obligated to play a vital role in their young communities. Indeed, for some women, the landscape itself strengthened their resolve to fulfill their moral duties. In 1872, Sister Blandina Segale journeyed from Ohio to Colorado and New Mexico to establish missions. "The immense expanse of the plains, the solid Rockies, the purity of the atmosphere, the faultlessness of the canopy above, will stretch the mind toward the Good," she wrote to another nun. "I wish I had many hands and feet, and a world full of hearts to place at the service of the Eternal."

Sister Blandina Segale, a native of Italy, and other members of the Sisters of Charity taught at the St. Joseph Convent in Trinidad, Colorado.

The frontier provided many ways for women to earn a livelihood while they also worked for the common good. Women started schools in their cabins or were dispatched by school boards to teach in designated regions. Women also cooked, sewed, and did laundry for others, especially for single men. Some women took in boarders or became innkeepers; others peddled produce from their gardens to earn extra money. Some women found more unusual forms of employment. Maggie Brown, of Rincon, New Mexico, slaughtered her own pigs and cured and sold the meat at market. Some women became trail guides, newspaper editors, or professional writers. Other women became successful ranchers or mine owners, either after their husbands had died or because they simply had better business skills than their spouses. And women doctors and lawyers also went west.

Women actively participated in politics as well. Mary E. Lease of Kansas and Luna Kellie of Nebraska both served as speakers and recruiters for their state chapters of the Farmers' Alliance and the Populist party, which was established in 1890. The Alliance developed programs to benefit farmers, including educational programs; associations for cooperative buying, marketing, and warehousing; and other strategies to improve farmers' economic status.

Its successor, the Populist party, converted these individual programs into a wide-ranging political platform designed to protect farmers' interests in an economy that catered increasingly to industrial and financial interests—"a government of Wall Street, by Wall Street, and for Wall Street," as Mary Lease bitingly declared. Both the Alliance and the Populist party recruited women as lecturers and organizers and supported woman suffrage. The Alliance, in particular, recognized the vital importance of rural women's economic activities and their keen interest in economic reforms that helped farmers.

Women also earned their livelihood in more dubious ways. In the mining camps of Butte, Montana, as well as in the desert outposts of New Mexico, women worked as prostitutes and owners of brothels and saloons. Women became prostitutes for a variety of reasons—to rebel against strict parents, to experience the adventure of a mining camp, or simply to earn a living when no other choice of work was available. Some women prospered and turned their earnings into lucrative real estate investments, but many women felt socially outcast and were at risk of contracting venereal diseases, which were often fatal, or of being physically abused by male customers.

The Becker sisters brand cattle on their ranch in Alamosa, Colorado. In the West, many women carved out successful livelihoods for themselves, including ranching.

Prostitution was a lonely, insecure life spent mostly in dark, shabby hotel rooms.

A shameful chapter in the settling of the West concerns Chinese women who were sold into prostitution. These unsuspecting young women were either kidnapped in China and smuggled into American ports, or they were deceived by agents posing as matchmakers who lured them to America. Either way, they became virtual slaves, forced to service the sexual needs of Chinese immigrant male laborers working on the railroads and ranches of the West. Some found sympathetic support from female missionaries who sheltered them in special group homes and trained them to be wives and mothers. But the missionaries pressured them into entering marriages that were not always happy or compatible, and these unfortunate young Chinese women still had little control over their lives.

Whether women worked directly on the land or in country schoolhouses and newspaper offices, nature's cruelty and its bounty had an indelible impact on their lives. Western farmers, ranchers, and miners relied on the kindness of nature to yield profitable crops, livestock, and minerals. A fire, flood, or illness could wipe out a family's livelihood. When Annie Green's husband contracted typhoid fever, she had to spend all of her time nursing him, and their crops went to ruin from neglect. Green was devastated. "Sinking to the earth, I wept and prayed to God for a change in my wretched life," she said.

Maggie and Charles Brown of Virginia moved back and forth across Colorado and New Mexico 24 times over 27 years in search of a better life. Between them, they had worked as physician, miner, carpenter, housepainter, farmer, mail clerk, poultry farmer, laundress, baker, and day servant. For a time, they prospered. But unyielding mines, drought, poor business sense, and sheer bad luck played havoc with their finances and their lives. They lost six children to illness, and by her mid-30s Maggie looked old and haggard. In a letter to her father, she confided, "I don't see any likelihood of times ever being any better. I feel if I do stay here two years longer I will be lost body and soul." Life on the land had decidedly not been kind to them.

Closely linked to how comfortable and secure women felt in their new homes was how trusting or distrusting they felt toward

Mary Lease, a fiery orator, was known as the Joan of Arc of the Kansas Populist movement. She urged farmers to "raise less corn and more Hell."

Chinese prostitutes in California catered to an eager clientele of ranchers and railroad workers. From 1852 to 1873, one Chinese secret society alone, the Hip-Yee Tong, imported 6,000 young women to the West Coast.

The Kansas Workman, *a weekly newspaper, employed female typesetters. Many newspaper owners found their women employees to be more adept at the fine, skilled work, and—perhaps because they were so active in the temperance movement—more reliable, too.*

native people who already lived there, such as Native Americans and Hispanics. Before embarking on the journey out west, travelers heard frightening stories about Indian attacks, especially on women and children. These stories preyed upon their fears and prejudices. Angeline Mitchell Brown of Arizona described an encounter with several Native American men who had broken into the cabin that she shared with two other women. Clearly frightened by this encounter, she gave full vent to all of her prejudices about Indians. Coming face to face with one of her invaders, she "looked at him then straight, & unflinchingly in his cruel gleaming eyes & I know I wondered if Satan in all his kingdom had a more fiendish looking devil."

In contrast, Mary Ronan, the wife of a government agent at the Flathead Indian Reservation in western Montana, claimed that she never shut or locked a door in her house and that Indians walked in anytime. But Ronan's trust and good feeling toward her Native American neighbors was tinged with condescension. Whenever she asked them to leave, she always gave them a little gift—"a bit of sugar, a piece of bread or an apple"—like a parent bribing a child with a treat. Most white men and women did not regard their Indian neighbors as equals. Instead, they condemned them as savages or treated them as exotic strangers or ignorant half-people needing instruction in the ways of white Christians. Even where friendships did occur, white settlers measured the friendship according to the standards of white civilization. As one Oklahoma woman settler said, the Indians "acted friendly and we found that they were as good as we were and couldn't help liking them."

Yet some white women managed to overcome cultural blinders and develop special friendships with Native American women. Indian women shared homemade remedies with white women or took them on expeditions to gather herbs and roots. Louise S. Gellhorn Boylan, an Iowa settler of the 1870s, "treasured greatly" some beads given to her by neighboring Indian women. And some white women eagerly attended Native American ceremonies and gatherings. White settlers also hired Native American men and women as domestics or nursemaids. From these employment arrangements emerged some friendships between employer and employee.

For their part, Native American women scorned white culture

for its materialism, disrespect for the land, and disregard for Native American culture. Although individual Indian women befriended white women and even married white men, Native American women had a long tradition of defending their people's birthright to their ancestral lands. As early as 1818, a delegation of Cherokee women vigorously urged their men to resist U.S. soldiers who were forcibly uprooting them from their homeland. In 1883, the eloquent Sarah Winnemucca pointed out the hypocrisy of a white society that called itself civilized but left a trail of blood as it invaded and plundered her people's homes.

Garden of Eden or land of desolation, good neighbor or savage, trusting white friend or invader—women's responses to the West and to one another were as varied as the terrain itself. Although women from all cultural backgrounds—Native American, Hispanic, white, and African-American—harbored fears and prejudices toward one another, friendships among individual women flourished as surely as the fragrant flowering desert cactus. More often, however, women from different backgrounds and races coexisted uneasily. But the common force in all of their lives was the land. There, before the white invader came, Native American women lovingly tended their stalks of corn and beans. Later on, other women came to use the land for different purposes, to wrest from the dusty soil their livelihood or their families' well-being and to build new communities and the foundations of a new life.

Presbyterian missionaries, austerely dressed in churchly finery, bring their message to an Apache camp in Oklahoma. White Christians particularly deplored the Native-American practice of wife swapping.

CHAPTER 5

"TO MAKE THE WHOLE WORLD HOMELIKE": WOMEN WORK TOGETHER FOR SOCIAL CHANGE

During the postwar years, women who lived in the dusty towns of Kansas as well as the burgeoning neighborhoods of New York City discovered new and different ways to make their voices heard and to enlarge the scope of their lives. Throughout the last three decades of the 19th century, a remarkable movement swept the country—women across the nation organized clubs to develop common interests and work together to improve their communities. Even before the Civil War, both white and free black women had organized associations to crusade against slavery or help less fortunate women in their own towns and cities. But after the war, a new surge of energy and interest among women ignited the creation of new, more ambitious clubs.

These clubs took various forms. Some were study clubs devoted to learning; others were fund-raising organizations designed to raise money for building schools, hospitals, orphanages, and other public institutions. In still other clubs, women became involved in local political causes or investigated working conditions in factories. Whatever the club's goals, its members seized the opportunity to enlarge their interests beyond their homes and families. In the process, they also challenged social practices and ideas about women's lives, although many women did not challenge their role as wives and mothers. Instead, they believed that their maternal concerns

The Women's Christian Temperance Union (WCTU) waged a formidable crusade against drinking, which this 1874 cartoon aptly titled "Woman's Holy War."

Journalist and magazine editor Jane Cunningham Croly sparked a nationwide club movement among American women when she established Sorosis, a club for professional women. Croly championed wider employment opportunities and financial independence for women.

obligated them to help improve the quality of life in their communities and neighborhoods.

In the postwar years, the first significant attempt to establish a women's club was Sorosis. In 1868, Jane Cunningham Croly, a journalist, organized the club in New York City after she was barred from attending a dinner hosted by the New York Press Club—of which she was a member—because she was a woman. Croly envisioned a group composed only of professional and other self-supporting women that, in her words, "should manage its own affairs, represent as far as possible the active interests of women, and create a bond of fellowship between them." After much debate, club members chose the name Sorosis, a botanical term for plants with a profusion of flowers that bear fruit. (The word *sorosis* comes from the Latin word *soror,* or "sister.") Members of Sorosis organized themselves into four groups—literature, art, drama, and music—and chose topics within those categories to study.

Most topics related in some way to women's lives. Although the club occasionally invited outside speakers, such as astronomer Maria Mitchell, members usually conducted the discussions themselves. According to their first president, Alice Cary, they aspired to teach themselves how to think more deeply and determine what subjects merited attention and debate. Sorosis meetings were not an occasion for "idle gossip," claimed Cary. But Sorosis members did not talk only about paintings and books. Throughout the club's existence, its guiding spirit, Jane Croly, urged members to study and act on reform issues from female labor to public sanitation and education. This philosophy is key to understanding the importance of Sorosis and other women's study clubs, for in offering women a forum for intellectual inquiry and discussion, these clubs urged women to first take their own ideas seriously and then to act upon those ideas.

Study clubs sprang up throughout the nation, especially in the Northeast and Midwest. Unlike Sorosis, these clubs were open to full-time homemakers as well as to professional and other wage-earning women. Like a spreading fever, women who visited friends and attended meetings of their clubs went home and established their own. The clubs' goals were as numerous as the clubs themselves. Some focused on several general subjects, such as art, literature, music, and politics; others focused on a single topic. The Great Expecta-

Following a lecture by Harvard professor Charles Copeland, members of Boston's Saturday Morning Club, costumed as Theban elders, enact the Greek play Antigone.

tions Club of Thomaston, Maine, studied English literature and history up to the Victorian era. The Portia Club of San Francisco, which had several women lawyers as members, endeavored to master principles of legal and political theory, and the Heliades Club of Chicago explored world geography.

The variety and range of topics within the study club movement were as wide as women's interests and desire to learn. In general, however, study clubs focused on literature, the arts, and history— subjects that members, most of whom lacked a formal education, had never had an opportunity to study. Many study clubs survived for a decade or more, and as their members gained greater self-confidence their critical thinking and writing skills greatly improved.

Study clubs, however, had their critics. In 1868, after Julia Ward Howe, author of the "Battle Hymn of the Republic" and an avid club woman herself, established the New England Women's Club, the *Boston Transcript* warned, "Homes will be ruined, children neglected, woman is straying from her sphere." But many club members had no intention of neglecting their domestic responsibilities. Instead, some women justified their club activities as ways to improve home and community life.

While attempting to quiet critics by emphasizing the value of clubs for home and family life, women also recognized the clubs' impact upon their own lives. They met women from different walks of life—older and younger women, professionals as well as full-time homemakers. Though study clubs were composed primarily of middle-class women and were seldom if ever integrated by race, members encountered a variety of life experiences and opinions different from their own. "I went to a Sorosis meeting the other day," declared one club woman. "And nothing ever impressed me so much. The fraternity, the versatility, and the spontaneity of those women was a revelation! A new life tingled through me from head to foot; my horizon broadens."

Study clubs offered many women exposure to new ideas, new friendships, and above all renewed respect for their own talents and abilities. As members gained new self-confidence and organizational skills, they looked beyond their own intellectual improvement to find ways to improve their communities. By the 1880s, many study clubs had begun to transform themselves into community service clubs. By 1889, for example, the Chicago Woman's Club, established in 1876 both to perform "practical work" and engage in intellectual study, had appointed a night matron in the city's prison and women physicians in the county insane asylum, introduced a system of kindergartens into Chicago's public school system, and

A volunteer from the National Council of Jewish Women (in white blouse, right) teaches English to young immigrant women.

established a school for male juvenile offenders.

Club women now expanded their domestic sense of responsibility to the entire community. They continued to feel their place was in the home, but home extended beyond the four walls of their private houses to the community.

The Woman's Christian Temperance Union (WCTU), established in 1874, reflected this idea of women as caretakers of their communities in its desire to ban alcohol. The WCTU started in Ohio when women embarked upon a campaign to close all of the saloons in the state. They identified alcohol as the source of family strife and the cause of immoral behavior in the home and community. Although temperance, or antiliquor, societies had existed before the Civil War, this latest effort to outlaw alcohol had spectacular success. Within several months, the women had closed down more than a thousand saloons and bars through prayer meetings, petitions, and intense pressure on customers and owners of bars.

Like the prewar abolition movement, this temperance crusade was a grass-roots effort that drew on religious precepts. Protection of the home and family from the irresponsible and violent behavior of men under the influence of alcohol was a moral and religious cause. Rebecca Felton of Georgia claimed that she joined the WCTU "because it represented organized Mother-love as opposed to this liquor curse." Like the study club movement, the temperance crusade ignited middle-class women's commitment, and the Woman's Christian Temperance Union rapidly grew in membership. Only women were eligible to join.

In 1879, after moving steadily up the leadership ranks, Frances Willard, a teacher from the Midwest, became the WCTU's energetic president. Willard infused new life into the WCTU. Under her leadership, the organization adopted new goals and strategies. She espoused a "Do Everything" policy, urging members to work to improve all aspects of women's lives. In 1884, she offered an explanation of her philosophy. Her words characterized the goal of other women's volunteer activities during this era: "Were I to define in a sentence, the thought and purpose of the Woman's Christian Temperance Union, I would reply: 'It is to make the whole world *homelike.*'"

Inspired by her vision, WCTU members worked not only for temperance but for a variety of causes. They created boys' and girls'

Rebecca Latimer Felton, a loyal member of the WCTU, became the first woman in the U.S. Senate in 1920. She told her colleagues, "When the women of the country come and sit with you, you will get ability, integrity of purpose, exalted patriotism, and unstinted usefulness."

Frances Willard may have been uncertain on a bicycle, but she was resolute in her leadership of the WCTU from 1879 to 1898.

clubs, homes for alcoholic women, and evening schools for working women. They also campaigned for better working conditions in factories, more humane prisons, health education in public schools, and public drinking fountains. But, Willard realized, the WCTU had no real power to bring about these changes until women could vote, and she made female enfranchisement a prime goal of the WCTU. "The Ballot for Home Protection," she declared, gave women their most potent weapon for combating the "tyranny of drink."

Women who had once opposed female enfranchisement became convinced of its necessity. Traditional in their outlook, they had once feared that female enfranchisement would, in their view, "unsex" women—that is, draw women away from their role in life as wives and mothers. To endorse female suffrage, then, was a dramatic step forward. But, to their new way of thinking, the ballot would not unsex women; instead, voting would help them carry out their moral mission as women more effectively because they now had the political power to implement temperance and other reforms.

The WCTU was only one of many women's organizations dedi-

cated to spreading the values of the home into the community. Another active organization was the Young Women's Christian Association (YWCA). Founded by middle-class women in Boston in 1867, the YWCA endeavored to assist young single women who had migrated from the farm to the city for work. The organization defined its goal to be the protection of the "temporal, moral, and religious welfare of young women who are dependent on their own exertions for support." To this end, YWCA representatives stationed themselves at bus and train depots, advising young women about employment opportunities and places to live. Eventually the YWCA established its own boardinghouses to ensure that women were living in morally respectable lodgings.

The Working Girls' Society was yet another attempt by middle-class women to be public mothers toward younger working-class women. Founded in 1885 by Grace Hoadley Dodge in New York City, the society attempted to instill proper middle-class values in working-class women. Club activities included lectures and group discussions on topics such as "Purity," "Womanhood," "How to Get a Husband,"

Among the activities offered to turn-of-the-century women by the YWCA were orchestras. In the first third of the 20th century, all-women's orchestras would offer opportunities to professional musicians who were not allowed to join established symphonies.

and "Money—How to Get It and Keep It." A few clubs maintained their own boardinghouses; these included libraries and classes in millinery and dressmaking, stenography, literature, physical education, and medical hygiene. By 1890, 75 chapters of the society had been established around the country. Dodge called the New York chapter a "home to all its members" and hoped that girls would learn the proper manners, form of dress, and language that their own parents had failed to teach them.

Dodge, who came from an affluent New York family active in charitable causes, hoped to persuade her charges that their true fulfillment lay in becoming genteel women like herself—"not desirous for man's work or place, but remaining where circumstances have placed them . . . developing and enlarging the power God has given them." But working-class members held fast to their own aspirations; they challenged Dodge's emphasis on a life of domesticity by insisting on their right to work and be financially independent.

American Jewish and African-American women established clubs as well. Jewish women, in particular, drew on religious values that enshrined women's special role as guardian of the Jewish home. In addition, they were also influenced by American middle-class perceptions of women's domestic role. By the 1870s, every sizable American Jewish community had a Ladies Temple Aid Society, Ladies Auxiliary, Passover Relief Fund, or Deborah and Leah lodges. These organizations raised money for local synagogues, assisted needy or ill Jewish women, helped find employment for Jewish newcomers, and assisted a growing influx of east European Jewish immigrants with housing and educational needs.

American Jewish women went about their club work quietly and deferred to the authority of rabbis and other male leaders. But these grass-roots volunteer organizations of the 1870s and 1880s served as a prelude to the emergence of a more comprehensive and ambitious program of political and social reform work initiated by Jewish women in the 1890s.

African-American women's clubs were often centered around their churches. Historically, black churches have provided solid support for their communities.

The National Council of Jewish Women, established in 1893, did more than organize local charity drives within Jewish neighborhoods. Its members educated themselves on public policy, testified before congressional committees, and tried to combat such social ills as poverty and juvenile delinquency within the Jewish commu-

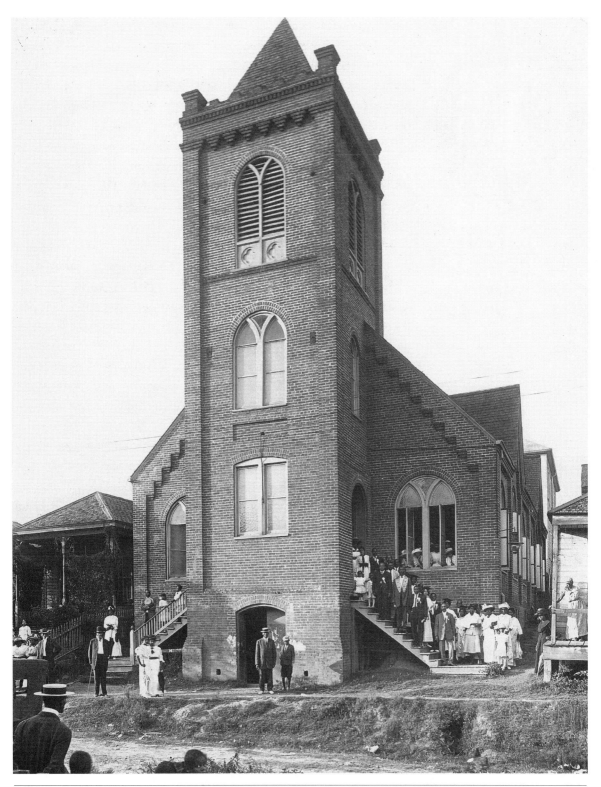

The logo of the National Council of Jewish Women, which incorporates the religious symbols of the Torah scroll and eternal light, also alludes to the organization's involvement in social welfare activities.

nity. Although the council expanded the sphere of Jewish women's volunteer concerns and voiced new ideas about female power and equality, its members did not challenge traditional notions about Jewish women's primary domestic role. Like the small, grass-roots Jewish organizations that preceded it, the council tried to expand the values of the home into the community.

African-American women also combined a desire to use their special gifts as women with an explicit aim to help their own people. And like the Jewish women's club movement, African-American women's club activities grew into a more ambitious program of social reform in the 1890s.

Many of these groups were affiliated with black churches. From the earliest days of Reconstruction, female members of the African Methodist Episcopal, Baptist, and Congregational churches organized ladies' benevolent societies. These groups hired physicians and teachers to serve the congregations of their own churches, provided financial aid to sick or impoverished church members, and raised funds for new church buildings and schools. Every black community had one or more women's benevolent societies, and these church-based groups guided their brethren through the difficult transition from bondage to freedom.

By the 1880s, however, African-American women were ready to help themselves, although they continued to perform volunteer services for their communities. In 1880, Mary Ann Shadd Cary and other black women organized the Colored Woman's Progressive Franchise Association. This was the first major organization created and led by black women. Although the association strove to help African-American women secure economic, political, and social equality for themselves, it also aimed to give black women the tools to help their own communities more effectively.

To this end, the association endorsed female suffrage. Like the WCTU, black women regarded the right to vote not as an abstract, universal right to which they were entitled as members of the human race, but as a powerful tool to improve their own lives and those of their people. Throughout the 1880s, African-American women pressed their claims for economic, social, and political equality, and they gradually entered professional fields. But central to their own sense of power was their obligation to their communities. In 1886,

Anna Julia Cooper, a black writer and educator, eloquently proclaimed this very idea. "Only the *Black Woman* can say 'when and where I enter . . . then and there the whole *Negro race enters with me.*'"

Within a few years, several prominent African-American women, including author and social worker Victoria Earle Matthews, physician Dr. Susan McKinney, and journalist and civic leader Josephine St. Pierre Ruffin, acted upon Cooper's vision. They organized clubs to improve the social, economic, and educational programs within their communities. In Atlanta, Georgia, for example, black women established a local Chautauqua study circle, using readings from the national adult education program of the same name based in Chautauqua, New York.

Besides implementing educational and social welfare programs, black women's clubs served another purpose: to disprove whites' racist views of black women as immoral and ignorant. These vicious prejudices had circulated since slavery. Between 1892 and 1894, African-American women's clubs sprang up throughout the nation, from the East Coast to the West. Through these clubs, which strove to improve educational and economic opportunities and strengthen family life in their communities, black women expressed their integrity, intellectual talents, and dedication to their people.

In the South, white women's club activity followed a somewhat different direction. Women also organized study clubs, and by the 1880s several Southern states had chapters of the Woman's Christian Temperance Union. The WCTU, however, had a harder time gaining a foothold in the South because of its support for woman suffrage. According to one Tennessee woman, even ministers opposed the WCTU! "They quote St. Paul," she remarked drily, "and tell us we are wonderfully out of our places."

Southern women organized other clubs as well. In New Orleans, clubs for working-class women helped them find employment and develop more marketable skills. Like the YWCA and other organizations for working-class women, the New Orleans Woman's Club, established in 1885, ran an employment bureau, which placed women in a variety of jobs, from teaching to office work and dressmaking.

In general, however, Southern white women's clubs were religious in aim and organization. Their club work often resembled the

Social worker Victoria Earle Matthews (top) established the White Rose Mission in New York City and was chairman of the executive board of the National Association of Colored Women. Susan McKinney, a physician, was a founder of the Woman's Loyal Union, the leading black women's club in New York, and of the Equal Suffrage League of Brooklyn.

activity of black women's church groups. Like African-American women, Southern white women organized clubs to raise funds for rebuilding churches and assisting destitute citizens. They also joined a movement then sweeping the nation, embracing both black and white women's church groups in its wake—foreign missionary work.

Between 1870 and 1910, female missionary societies from across the nation sent missionaries throughout the world to spread the gospel of Christianity. They transformed the foreign-missionary movement into a systematic program of fund-raising and education. Local missionary societies for each religious denomination organized into federations, and each federation published a magazine that offered detailed accounts about the geography and social customs of the foreign countries to which missionaries were sent. These federations, however, were not integrated—black women's missionary societies remained separate from those of white women.

But black and white female missionary societies shared similar concerns, especially in regard to the status of women in non-Christian countries. They decried the inadequate education, social isolation, and harsh treatment that they perceived to be the plight of foreign women. Amanda Smith, an African-American missionary in Liberia, observed, "There is so little attention paid to the education of girls; not a single high school for girls in the whole republic of Liberia. It is a great shame and a disgrace to the government."

Female missionaries also deplored certain cultural practices that physically harmed women, such as foot-binding in China. Although their concerns were based on fact, they glorified the treatment of women and girls in the United States by contrast, without questioning the hard lot of many women in this country. Some of their concerns, however, such as protecting women and girls from heavy physical labor, found their way into the social programs of reformers in America who opposed child labor and lobbied for better working conditions and higher wages for American women.

Although some women extended the values of the home into the community, and also abroad, other women brought the community into the home. In 1889, Jane Addams and Ellen Gates Starr established Hull House in a poor immigrant neighborhood in Chicago. In the same year, Vida Scudder, an English professor at Wellesley College, and six other women rented a tenement building in New York

City's Lower East Side, a community composed mostly of Jewish immigrants from eastern Europe. They named their settlement house the College Settlement Association. The settlement house movement had begun. Trained workers lived in both settlement houses and taught local residents cooking, sewing, hygiene, and English. They also provided day care for children of working mothers. In addition, settlement houses began to play a more political role by providing meeting places for trade unions or helping to settle labor disputes between employers and employees.

Settlement houses drew young college-educated women workers who aspired to improve the living and working conditions of poor people. They believed that, with the proper assistance, people could help themselves. By living and working in crowded immigrant neighborhoods, they hoped to bridge a growing economic and cultural gap between rich and poor and share in the community life of local residents. Mary McDowell, a settlement worker, expressed the idealism behind the settlement house movement: "Here was something I had been looking for all my life, a chance to work with the least skilled workers in our greatest industry; not for them as a missionary, but with them as a neighbor and seeker after truth."

Although settlement workers confronted appalling poverty in these tenement neighborhoods, they achieved modest gains in help-

Episcopal missionaries to a Chippewa reservation in Minnesota teach the Indian women to make lace. Missionary work was a way for middle-class women to move out of the home into the larger world.

Immigrants living in Chicago found a warm welcome at Hull House, the settlement house founded by Jane Addams and Ellen Starr. At right, Starr, a volunteer, and Addams enjoy a tea break.

ing people improve their lives. By 1906, 17 years after Hull House and the College Settlement Association opened their doors, nearly 200 settlement houses existed in the United States, staffed mostly by women who, like club women, desired to improve community life.

Women also brought their maternal values to bear on a subject of great concern for all women—birth control. Prior to 1873, women could learn about ways to regulate reproduction through advertisements in women's and general-interest magazines. But in 1873, access to birth control information was dealt a severe blow when Congress passed the Comstock Act. Named after Anthony Comstock, secretary of the New York Society for the Suppression of Vice, the law prohibited selling, distributing, or mailing obscene literature. The Comstock Act expressly defined all contraceptive devices, and any information about them, as obscene. It also forbade any birth control advertisements in magazines, newspapers, books, and other forms of reading material.

The law reflected a pervasive belief that both contraception and abortion thwarted a divinely inspired plan of procreation. Comstock was commissioned as a special agent of the Post Office Department to help enforce the provisions of the law named after him. Between 1873 and 1880, he and his associates zealously pursued and helped to indict 55 persons whom Comstock identified as abortionists.

But an unusual coalition of reformers from many causes got around

this law by advocating a form of birth control that gave women the right to say no to their husbands' sexual advances. These advocates argued that a woman had the right to decide when to bear a child. In this way, women would bear healthier, happier children because they were willing and able to care for those children. Far from advocating a woman's freedom to have sex whenever she wished, supporters of "voluntary motherhood," as it was called, argued that women must have the freedom not to have sex and that husbands cannot impose their sexual will on their wives.

Advocates of voluntary motherhood represented a range of causes and points of view: They included feminists, such as Elizabeth Cady Stanton, who strongly affirmed women's right to reject men's sexual advances; free-love advocates, who opposed legal marriage because it stifled true love; and conservative religious crusaders who opposed woman suffrage but endorsed voluntary motherhood as a way to restrict "sexual excess."

There is no way of knowing to what extent women successfully relied upon the strategy of voluntary motherhood to regulate their sexual relations. Law and custom upheld men's right to demand

Mothers pose proudly with their daughters at Boston's Denison House, a settlement house modeled after Jane Addams's Hull House. Nurses employed by such organizations taught new mothers how to care for their babies.

Elizabeth Cady Stanton with her daughter Harriot in 1856. Stanton emphasized her experience as a mother when trying to win support for the woman suffrage movement.

sexual relations with their wives. But women found ways to control the number of children that they bore. From 1800 to 1900, the birthrate among American women declined by about one half. In 1800, the average birthrate was 7.04 children for every married woman; by 1900, it had dropped to 3.56. Between 1860 and 1910, the number of children born to white women dropped by about one-third, from 5.21 to 3.42. Exact figures are not available for African-American women; for the period between 1880 to 1910, however, the birthrate among black women also declined by about one-third. This dramatic decline in birthrates suggests that American women were using new forms of contraception, such as douches, pessaries, and suppositories, and also abortion. Condoms for men also became more widely available by the 1880s because of the invention of the vulcanization of rubber.

But contraception techniques were not always reliable, especially when people were not adept at using them correctly, and women resorted to abortions. Among physicians there was growing opposition to abortion on moral grounds, and the Comstock Act prohibited advertising for all forms of birth control, including abortion. Nevertheless, from about 1840 to 1880 physicians and public health officials reported a rising number of abortions among American women, especially middle-class married women. No doubt, more cases went unreported—especially among working-class women who could not afford the cost of an abortion and resorted to homemade and often tragically dangerous methods of ending a pregnancy. In 1858, the price of an abortion ranged from $25 to $60. By the 1870s, the price had fallen to about $10. Still, $10 was a hefty amount for a domestic or female factory hand who was barely surviving on her meager wages.

Clearly, then, both black and white women relied on new forms of birth control and also abortion to limit the number of children they bore. To what extent women adopted the precepts of voluntary motherhood as a form of birth control cannot be determined. But voluntary motherhood was an important first step toward recognizing women's right to control their reproduction, even if they did not yet have the social or legal power to act on that right. Sexual intercourse in the late 19th century carried many risks, including venereal disease, pregnancy, and childbirth—all potentially life-threatening results that could profoundly alter a woman's life. Any step toward giving women greater ability to regulate their sexual and reproductive activities also gave them a measure of control over their lives.

In many ways, then, American women eagerly tried to improve their lives and communities. In addition, they attempted to improve their own homes. The postwar years ushered in an array of labor-saving conveniences, such as electricity, running water, refrigerators, washing machines, cream separators, and processed and canned foods. But operating some of these devices, such as hand-cranked washing machine wringers and boilers, was still time-consuming, and many women could not afford these new contraptions. Nor did all households, especially homes in rural areas and less affluent families, have access to electricity or running water. In the 1870s and 1880s, many women still spent long days doing their own sewing, washing, and cooking.

Catharine Beecher, who had earlier proposed ways to help women manage their homes, continued in the late 1860s to devise methods for both simplifying and dignifying housework. In 1869, she and her sister Harriet Beecher Stowe published a book entitled *The American Woman's Home*, a guide to creating the ideal American

Washing machines and other new technology helped relieve women of some of the drudgery of housework. This device was meant to replace the washboard and open tub and could be operated neatly even by women wearing fancy clothes.

home. They included detailed floor plans showing careful organization of work space and appliances for cooking and laundry and urged readers to use the most advanced household technology to save time and create a cleaner, more comfortable home. They even indicated where knickknacks and pictures should be displayed to their best advantage.

Aware that women lived both in cities and on farms, the Beecher sisters offered both rural and urban variations of this ideal home, and went on to describe a "Model Christian Neighborhood." In this idealized village, 10 to 12 families shared the services of a commercial bakery and laundry so that homemakers were not burdened by the chores of doing laundry or baking bread. Neither Catharine nor Harriet Beecher questioned women's domestic role. Instead, they hoped to strengthen women's control over their households and endow the homemaker's role with greater respect, dignity, and proficiency.

Other women developed an even more cooperative vision of homemaking. In 1868, Melusina Fay Peirce, a housewife from Cambridge, Massachusetts, decided that she had had enough of "the dusty drudgery of house ordering." She proposed that women organize cooperative associations to share the task of doing housework in buildings equipped for such purposes. She also proposed that they charge their husbands for their services. Peirce suggested that all

The New Housekeeper's Manual by Catharine Beecher and Harriet Beecher Stowe, published in 1873, provided floor plans for efficient houses. Fuel was stored near the furnace, linens near the laundry, and living quarters were on the first floor, above the work space.

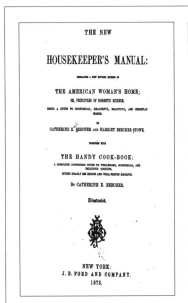
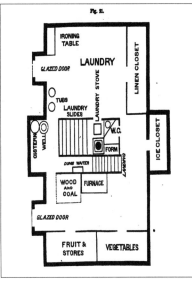
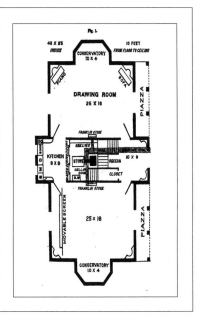

The November 1889 issue of Cosmopolitan *magazine ran side-by-side pictures contrasting an immaculate cooperative laundry with the relative chaos of a tenement washday.*

members be paid wages out of the fees that they collected from their husbands and that they charge competitive retail prices for cooked meals, laundry, and sewing—cash on delivery. Peirce had two goals in mind: to compensate homemakers for their labor and to free them from long days of household drudgery so that they could pursue other interests.

To put her ideas into practice, Peirce organized her own association, the Cambridge Cooperative Housekeeping Society, in May 1869. It eventually failed, however, because of members' lack of commitment and men's opposition. But Peirce's ideas spurred other thinkers to develop ways to make domestic life less exploitive and time-consuming. She believed that women must earn their own living and organize among themselves in order to lead happy, productive lives.

Marie Stevens Howland, a former mill worker, carried Peirce's vision of cooperative homemaking even further. Howland envisioned cooperative communities in which women found paid employment in fields other than housework. These communities would also provide professional child care and housekeeping services—cooking, cleaning, and laundry—for working mothers. Howland wrote two novels about her ideas and helped organize an experimental community in Mexico.

Like Peirce, Howland believed that women must be financially independent. She was among the first American women to challenge the sanctity of the nuclear family—a mother, a father, and their children living in a separate household—and to urge both men and women to find more than one sexual partner. She envisioned a community in which women were free to work at any job without worrying about cooking and cleaning and taking care of their children, because all of these services would be available to them.

Working-class women were also organizing to fight bread-and-butter battles for fair wages. In 1868, the Working Women's Protective Union was established to fight for higher wages and shorter working hours. All working women, except household servants, were eligible to join the Working Women's Protective Union. The union helped working-class women collect unpaid wages from dishonest employers, ran an employment bureau, and tried to develop new kinds of jobs for women. The New York branch of the Working Women's Protective Union collected thousands of dollars in unpaid wages for women and placed 1,500 to 2,000 women in jobs each year. In 1883, its director noted, "We do not give shelter, and we do not give charity. We furnish employment and we furnish advice and protection and open, as far as we can, avenues of labor to women."

But working-class women wanted more than protection—they sought justice on the job as well. To this end, they joined or formed their own unions to represent their interests as workers. The Daughters of St. Crispin, a union of female shoemakers, became the first national labor union of women workers in the United States. At the first meeting in Lynn, Massachusetts, on July 28, 1869, 30 delegates represented 11 lodges, or chapters, from cities as far away as San Francisco and Chicago. They demanded equal pay for equal work, but they softened their demand by assuring that equal pay would make them better homemakers. Over the next two years, they participated in two strikes for higher wages. They lost one and won the other. But a severe economic depression in 1873 halted all of their activity. Workers were so desperate to keep their jobs that they curtailed union activism that antagonized employers.

Elsewhere, women workers also left their jobs and went on strike for higher wages, with mixed results. Sometimes they won their demands, and sometimes they lost. Still, despite setbacks on the picket lines, women workers clearly demonstrated their ability to organize themselves and demand better wages and working conditions.

Early attempts at organizing unions paved the way for women's entry into two major labor unions: the Knights of Labor, in 1879, and the American Federation of Labor (AFL), in 1886. The Knights

Lawyers from the Working Women's Protective Union hear a complaint against a sewing machine operator. The WWPU tried to protect working women from unfair and exploitive employers.

of Labor was the first major labor union to actively recruit both white women and African-American men and women. Even house-wives were eligible for membership.

Although only 2 percent of women workers—approximately 50,000 female wage-earners—ever joined the Knights during its peak years of activity, the organization fought for equal pay for equal work by men and women. A permanent women's committee was established to investigate any wage inequities between men and women workers. The Knights also emphasized cooperatives, much like Melusina Fay Peirce's vision of cooperative housekeeping, in which women workers joined together to provide a service or a product rather than work for someone else. This working arrangement ap-

In 1886 these women were the first female delegates to the Knights of Labor. Elizabeth Rodgers, a delegate from Chicago, who rose rapidly in the leadership ranks of the Knights of Labor, holds her two-week-old son. The Knights opened its membership to some 270 women's locals and more than 100 "mixed" locals.

pealed to women workers, and a number of cooperatives operated by women arose. The Knights of Labor appealed to the interests and needs of working women who desired equal wages but recognized women's homemaking responsibilities as well.

But several factors brought about the demise of the Knights of Labor. These included unsuccessful strikes, financial problems from investing in cooperatives that failed, an embattled and inept leadership, and growing competition for workers' loyalties from the emerging American Federation of Labor. By the late 1880s, the Knights of Labor no longer commanded the loyalty of most working-class women and men.

Women received a less enthusiastic welcome from the American Federation of Labor (AFL), a loosely knit body of independent national and international unions that reached out primarily to skilled workers. Women workers in industry generally held jobs that required no special skills or training. For the first few years, women actually felt unwelcome at AFL meetings, which were held at night, when most women did household chores. Sometimes women could not afford the membership dues. When they received a discount on their membership they also received fewer benefits and fewer opportunities to speak out on union matters. By 1890, however, women workers began to demand more recognition in the AFL.

They fought an uphill battle because the AFL, unlike the Knights of Labor, refused to acknowledge that women were wage-earners as well as wives and mothers. Their traditional perceptions of women's roles blinded them to the growing numbers—and militancy—of women workers. By the early 20th century, women factory workers, especially those who worked in the garment industry, had proved willing to put their jobs and lives at risk to protest their low wages and intolerable working conditions. Eventually, the AFL recognized women workers' commitment to the goals of unionizing and began to recruit more women workers for membership.

In the last three decades of the 19th century, American women were discovering the power of collective action—to educate themselves, to improve their communities and crusade for suffrage and other rights, to seek fair wages and better working conditions, and to make housework in the private household less time-consuming and odious. Women were coming together, even as greater class barriers, sectional and political loyalties, and philosophical differences regarding women's social roles undermined any kind of unified outlook. Although Northern and Southern women still harbored some resentments and sectional loyalties from the Civil War, they were meeting each other more frequently on the common ground of national political and club activity.

The National American Woman Suffrage Association united women from around the country into one organized campaign for female enfranchisement. In 1890, the same year that the National American Woman Suffrage Association was organized, women who were members of individual clubs came together to form the Gen-

The emblem of the General Federation of Women's Clubs includes a sunburst with rays of light. This universal symbol in the women's movement was meant to represent the dawn of a new day.

eral Federation of Women's Clubs. Mary Eastman, a member of the New England Women's Club, expressed the underlying goal of the federation: "We must learn sympathy, learn unity, learn the great lesson of organization. . . . These clubs have made a new world, and we have got to adapt ourselves to it and to educate the world around us."

But the unity and sympathy of the General Federation of Women's Clubs had its limits; the federation refused to admit African-American women's clubs to its membership rolls. Six years later, black women forged their own chain of unity by organizing the National Association of Colored Women, a federation of African-American women's clubs, to share ideas and goals and work more effectively for the betterment of their people.

Not only did women from around the country begin to meet on common ground, but women from the Old World of eastern and southern Europe and the New World of the United States were also discovering shared concerns and interests. The 1880s and 1890s witnessed a massive influx of immigrants from Europe to America's shores. From Russia and Romania, Italy, Bohemia, Austria, and elsewhere almost 9 million came in search of a better life. Some American women were arrogant and distrusting toward the immigrants, dismissing them as inferior foreigners. Others hoped to strip them of their Old World ways and remake them into model Americans. But other American women overcame their arrogance and suspicions, and they genuinely welcomed their immigrant sisters to their new country. Over the coming decades, in the labor movement, in

local volunteer associations, and in the suffrage campaign, immigrant and native-born American women even worked together toward the same goal: political and economic justice for women.

Peering into the future, Antoinette Brown Blackwell, the visionary women's rights activist, observed in 1875, "It is a general impulse, and one of those tidal waves in social life, which is impelling so many women into such varied fields of activity. What influence is powerful enough to arrest it?" As American women from across the country strode toward the 20th century, bringing with them different hopes and visions of women's lives, they surely wondered what indeed could possibly hold them back from joining that vast tidal wave of activity.

Members of the National Council of Jewish Women meet immigrants as they arrive at Ellis Island. The NCJW's Americanization program helped them find housing and jobs, learn English, and otherwise adapt to life in the New World.

CHRONOLOGY

April 9, 1865	Civil War ends
April 14, 1865	President Lincoln assassinated
December 6, 1865	13th Amendment to the Constitution ratified; outlaws slavery
1865	American Equal Rights Association organized Vassar College founded
1867	Congress abolishes treaties with Native Americans and establishes reservation system
July 9, 1868	14th Amendment to the Constitution ratified; affirms U.S. citizenship status of all native-born or naturalized Americans, including African Americans
September 1868	Susan B. Anthony organizes the Working Woman's Association
1868	Working Women's Protective Union organized Sorosis organized
May 1869	Elizabeth Cady Stanton and Susan B. Anthony form the National Woman Suffrage Association
May 10, 1869	The transcontinental railroad completed at Promontory Point, Utah
July 1869	Daughters of St. Crispin organized; first national labor union for women
November 1869	Lucy Stone and Henry Blackwell organize the American Woman Suffrage Association
February 3, 1870	15th Amendment to the Constitution ratified; protects voting rights of African-American men
1870	Woman suffrage passed in Wyoming and Utah territories
1873	Comstock Law passed; bans the sale or mailing of all literature considered obscene, including birth control information
1874	Woman's Christian Temperance Union formed Harvard Annex opened
1875	Smith and Wellesley Colleges founded
1880	Colored Woman's Progressive Franchise Association organized Women join the Knights of Labor
1884	Bryn Mawr College founded

1886	Women join the American Federation of Labor
1889	Barnard College founded Hull House and College Settlement Association founded
December 29, 1890	Massacre of Sioux Indian tribe at Wounded Knee, South Dakota
1890	National American Woman Suffrage Association organized General Federation of Women's Clubs organized

The Methodist Episcopal Ladies Aid Society in Cincinnati, Ohio, ran a soup kitchen that provided needy citizens with warm meals.

FURTHER READING

A Note on Sources

In the interest of readability, the volumes in this series include no discussion of historiography and no footnotes. As works of synthesis and overview, however, they are greatly indebted to the research and writing of other historians. The principal works drawn on in this volume are among the books listed below.

General Histories of Women

Evans, Sarah M. *Born for Liberty: A History of Women in America*. New York: Free Press, 1989.

Jones, Jacqueline. *Labor of Love, Labor of Sorrow: Black Women, Work, and the Family from Slavery to the Present*. New York: Basic Books, 1985.

Kessler-Harris, Alice. *Out to Work: A History of Wage-Earning Women in the United States*. New York: Oxford University Press, 1982.

Scott, Anne Firor. *The Southern Lady: From Pedestal to Politics*. Chicago: University of Chicago Press, 1970.

Solomon, Barbara. *In the Company of Educated Women: A History of Women and Higher Education in America*. New Haven, Conn.: Yale University Press, 1985.

Sterling, Dorothy, ed. *We Are Your Sisters*. New York: Norton, 1984.

Wertheimer, Barbara Mayer. *We Were There: The Story of Working Women in America*. New York: Pantheon, 1977.

19th-Century History

Avary, Myrta Lockett. *Dixie After the War*. New York: Da Capo, 1970.

Banner, Lois W. *Elizabeth Cady Stanton: A Radical for Woman's Rights*. Boston: Little, Brown, 1980.

Bleser, Carol, ed. *In Joy and in Sorrow: Women, Family, and Marriage in the Victorian South, 1830–1900*. New York: Oxford University Press, 1991.

Boardman, Fon W., Jr. *America and the Gilded Age, 1876–1900*. New York: Henry Z. Walck, 1972.

Braude, Ann. *Radical Spirits: Spiritualism and Women's Rights in Nineteenth-Century America*. Boston: Beacon Press, 1989.

Brown, Dee. *Bury My Heart at Wounded Knee*. New York: Holt, Rinehart & Winston, 1991.

Clark, Judith Freeman. *America's Gilded Age: An Eyewitness History*. New York: Facts on File, 1992.

Clinton, Catherine. *The Other Civil War: American Women in the Nineteenth Century*. New York: Hill & Wang, 1984.

Cooper, Ilene. *Susan B. Anthony*. New York: Franklin Watts, 1984.

Fox, Mary Virginia. *Lady for the Defense: A Biography of Belva Lockwood*. New York: Harcourt Brace Jovanovich, 1978.

Giddings, Paula. *When and Where I Enter: The Impact of Black Women on Race and Sex in America.* New York: William Morrow, 1984.

Hayden, Dolores. *The Grand Domestic Revolution.* Cambridge, Mass.: MIT Press, 1981.

Hilton, Suzanne. *The Way It Was—1876.* Philadelphia: Westminster Press, 1975.

Jensen, Joan, ed. *With These Hands: Women Working on the Land.* Old Westbury, N.Y.: Feminist Press, 1981.

Kraditor, Aileen S., ed. *Up from the Pedestal: Selected Writings in the History of American Feminism.* New York: Quadrangle/ New York Times Book Co., 1968.

Lerner, Gerda, ed. *Black Women in White America.* New York: Vintage, 1973.

MacDonald, Anne L. *Feminine Ingenuity: Women and Invention in America.* New York: Ballantine Books, 1992.

Martin, Theodora Penny. *The Sound of Our Own Voices: Women's Study Clubs, 1860–1910.* Boston: Beacon Press, 1987.

Massey, Mary Elizabeth. *Bonnet Brigades.* New York: Knopf, 1966.

Meigs, Cornelia. *Jane Addams: Pioneer for Social Justice.* Boston: Little, Brown, 1970.

Mohrs, James C., ed. *The Cormany Diaries: A Northern Family in the Civil War.* Pittsburgh: University of Pittsburgh Press, 1982.

Moynihan, Ruth B., Susan Armitage, and Christiane Fischer Dichamp, eds. *So Much to Be Done: Women Settlers on the Mining and Ranching Frontier.* Lincoln: University of Nebraska Press, 1990.

Myers, Sandra L. *Westering Women and the Frontier Experience: 1800–1915.* Albuquerque: University of New Mexico Press, 1982.

Reiter, Joan Swallow, and the editors of Time-Life Books. *The Women.* The Old West series. Alexandria, Va.: Time-Life Books, 1978.

Sklar, Kathryn Kish. *Catharine Beecher: A Study in American Domesticity.* New Haven, Conn.: Yale University Press, 1973.

Weiner, Lynn. *From Working Girl to Working Mother: The Female Labor Force in the United States, 1820–1980.* Chapel Hill: University of North Carolina Press, 1985.

Werstein, Irving. *This Wounded Land: The Era of Reconstruction, 1865–1877.* New York: Delacorte, 1968.

Western Writers of America. *The Women Who Made the West.* Garden City, N.Y.: Doubleday, 1980.

Whicher, George Frisbie. *This Was a Poet: A Critical Biography of Emily Dickinson.* 1938. Reprint. Hamden, Conn.: Archon Books, 1980.

Woodward, C. Vann. *Mary Chesnut's Civil War.* New Haven, Conn.: Yale University Press, 1981.

Fiction

Beatty, Patricia. *Be Ever Hopeful, Hannalee.* Mahwah, N.J.: Troll, 1988.

Conrad, Pam. *Prairie Songs.* New York: Harper Trophy, 1985.

Lasky, Kathryn. *The Bone Wars.* New York: Puffin, 1988.

Traver, Robert. *Laughing Whitefish.* New York: McGraw-Hill, 1965.

Walker, Margaret. *Jubilee.* New York: Bantam, 1967.

Wilder, Laura Ingalls. Little House Series. New York: HarperCollins Children's Books.

Acknowledgments

I wish to thank several people for their generous assistance in helping me to complete this book. My former dissertation adviser, Professor Joyce Avrech Berkman, started me on the journey that has led to this book, and her dedication to scholarship in women's history continues to inspire my own. Professor Nancy Cott kindly gave me the opportunity to write this volume, and to her I extend a special thank-you. Both she and Nancy Toff, executive editor at Oxford University Press, carefully read various drafts of the manuscript and their astute comments greatly improved the book. In addition, Ms. Toff and Paul McCarthy, her assistant, good-naturedly dealt with the formidable task of getting this book off of my computer system and onto theirs, and Tara Deal, project editor, skillfully guided the book through its many stages of production.

On a more personal note there are numerous people whom I wish to thank for their sustaining encouragement: my husband, Jay Banks, to whom I joyfully dedicate this volume; my father, Leon Sigerman, and my brother, Jon Sigerman; my father-in-law, Ephraim Banks; and the very special women in my life: my sister, Lynn Hill; my honorary sister-in-law, Nancy Stifel; my honorary mothers, Jean Colbert, Estelle Kastleman, and Helen Steinberg; and my dearest friends—who have been like sisters through the years—Lori Burns, Pamela Lasky, Shelly Perron, Jessie Rodrique, and Joan Tomczyk.

Picture Credits

INDEX

Harriet Sigerman is a freelance historian and writer who has contributed to *European Immigrant Women in the United States: A Biographical Dictionary* and *The Young Reader's Companion to American History*. She has been a research assistant to Henry Steele Commager at Amherst College and for the Stanton-Anthony Papers at the University of Massachusetts at Amherst. A graduate of the University of California at Irvine, she holds an M.A. and Ph.D. in American history from the University of Massachusetts at Amherst.

Nancy F. Cott is Stanley Woodward Professor of history and American studies at Yale University. She is the author of *The Bonds of Womanhood: "Woman's Sphere" in New England 1780–1835*; *The Grounding of Modern Feminism*; and *A Woman Making History: Mary Ritter Beard Through Her Letters*, editor of *Root of Bitterness: Documents of the Social History of American Women*, and co-editor of *A Heritage of Her Own: Towards a New Social History of American Women*.